The Great Art Hoax

The Great Art Hoax
Essays in the Comedy and Insanity of Collectible Art

Jon Huer

Bowling Green State University Popular Press
Bowling Green, Ohio 43403

Library of Congress Catalogue Card No.: 90-080919

ISBN: 087972-491-9 cb
     087972-492-7 pb

Cover design by Gary Dumm

To
Jonathan Blake Huer
with love

Contents

Chapter 1

Wherefore Art Thou?

Not too long ago, I attended a well publicized modern art exhibition sponsored by a large university in North Carolina. The exhibition featured de Kooning, Rauschenberg, Lichtenstein, and other Who's Who of modern art, including Andy Warhol. While at the gallery trying desperately to hide my incapacity to comprehend many of the artworks, I was attracted to one particular painting in the collection, a relatively large work entitled "Grayed Yellow Vertical Rectangle," done by an artist named Jo Baer.

This is what the accompanying description, obviously written by an expert who supplied it as an added explanation for the artwork, said in part: "...A flat white (or very pale gray) painted canvas with a narrow black border either intricately broken by fine color lines in the upper, heavier margin, or evenly lined with a narrower inner border of grayed (though often intense) color—a luminescent shadow rather than a direct contrast. This inner border serves as a binding agent for the whole painting. It mediates the encounter of dark edge and light field, while adding an almost imperceptible tension; and it deters the white center from recoiling into space and becoming a window."

What particularly aroused my curiosity was the fact that the large canvas had appeared to have nothing painted on it. IT WAS BLANK! It was just a white painted canvas, as though the artist had gotten the canvas ready for her artwork but then completely forgotten to paint anything. The "whole painting" that the expert spoke of was in fact "no painting" at all, nothing but a large, empty canvas. But in view of the elaborate description supplied by this art expert about this nothing and the simple fact that it was on display *as* art, it was or became something. No art was there that I could see, but it was obviously there for all to see.

Was it art because it was exhibited and collected, or was it exhibited and collected because it was art? Something did not stand to reason, and I decided to pursue these and other questions. What my relentless pursuit has eventually led me to, even surprising to myself, is the subject of this book.

Let me then state what this book is all about in summary form: Never has there been a greater mixture of comedy and insanity in an institution than that displayed in the Art Establishment. The discovery has left me in a fairly devastating frame of mind, especially after having written a scholarly book in defense of art. Besides, no one likes to give up a comfortable myth, especially one as deeply entrenched in our consciousness as art. The only consolation may be that, although much of "art" has been lost in the discovery of its unreality, much truth about art has been gained in its place.

When the subject is art, and especially the kind of art that is really *no art*, as in the encounter above, people are inclined to display either one of the following two responses. They pretend to know something about it although they know nothing about it—even when there is *nothing* to know. Or they confess to knowing nothing about it and proceed to apologize for their ignorance, even though what they know nothing about is literally *nothing*. It seems to me it is only in art that many people feel they should know *something*, even when there *is* nothing to know. Art, as one of its magical powers and mysteries, tends to have this sort of influence, even over reasonably intelligent people.

But this confusion is true of certain art, not all art. To be clear about this, let me mention the two kinds of art forms that I use in this book: "Uncollectible" art and "collectible" art. This pair—although already established as the art market's standard practice—is still an unfamiliar classification. But I believe this collectible-uncollectible dichotomy cuts straight to the heart of the art business better than anything else. In the world of art and art value, the key question always is whether Artwork X is "collectible" or not, and at what price. All else is unimportant. Even experts confess that they cannot precisely define art, but that does not keep artworks from selling at a precise price.

The simple fact of whether something is collectible or not determines everything else that follows. Say anything you want about the "beauty," "elegance," "aesthetic value," or whatever of art, the single most important truth about art is still this one: CAN I OWN IT? If artworks couldn't be collected, art couldn't exist. To love art is to own it. Art exists because of collection, not in itself. But what is considered most important in art today—collecting—is the most *un*important part of art. For art and collecting—inseparable as they are in today's vocabulary— have nothing in common.

Art has traditionally been divided into "major" and "minor" art. The former includes all established art forms, such as literature, painting, music; the latter includes crafts, decoration, furniture, folk art, and so on. But this division, although widely used, really tells us nothing about the difference between the forms. What is major and minor art, and why is it major or minor? Of course, we cannot say, other than that the distinction is conventional. But we can answer these questions if we switch to the new classification: Anything is major art if it is collected with major money. Minor art, conversely, is an art form that is either uncollected or collected with only minor money. As far as the art world is concerned, art that is not collected is not art. Collectible art is valued because, once placed in someone's collection, the whole artwork belongs to its owner; copies or imitations—no matter how good—are considered irrelevant and unworthy of collection.

But certain artworks are uncollectible. No one can *exclusively* collect any opus in music, literature, philosophy, or drama, so that no one else can have access to it. Unlike collectible art, uncollectible art is public. People go to see Shakespeare's plays, buy and listen to Beethoven's recordings, and. read inexpensive copies of great novels without interference from anyone and with only a cursory glance in the direction of experts and collectors. Few people with a complete set of Shakespeare's plays, Beethoven's symphonies, or the great American novels would ever call them "my art collection." People purchase these works simply because they enjoy them. Uncollectible artworks are virtually worthless as collections. In these art forms, art and collection have no imperative connection; they are wholly independent of each other. Such art forms represent "free art," art free from privatization by collectors. There are just too many copies of these artworks for them to be wholly owned by one collector. Hence they are uncollectible.

Collectible art forms, unlike uncollectible, have no public audience in the true sense of the term. Too many intermediaries stand between these forms and their public: There are art galleries that select and display the works; there are art critics who make pronouncements about the works on display; there are art dealers who match buyers with appropriate artworks; there are auction houses whose gavel instantly immortalizes or obliterates the works; and then there are artist-businessmen whose customers happen to be art collectors. The business remains just too mysterious and forbidding for ordinary people to comprehend.

All of the art business is thus concerned with collecting. In fact, collecting is the *only* business of collectible art: Finding something to collect; selling and buying the collectible; making insignificant things into significant collectibles; publicizing the collections; creating competition among collectors.

What is indeed collected as art? Anything and everything. When asked what art is, Picasso gave his famous answer: "What isn't?" Indeed, what isn't art and what isn't collectible? This question is the ultimate invitation to comedy and insanity. By the time an artwork (or non-artwork) goes through dealers, experts, and collectors, nothing has become something and something nothing, all depending on who collects it and for how much. It is this strange process that mystifies art and terrifies ordinary people.

How shall we demystify art and unmask the comedy and insanity that are the art business?

Social scientists know that most important clues to any phenomenon can be found in studying its "opposite." To better understand Democrats, we simply talk to Republicans, and vice versa. To have a better angle on American society, we look at Soviet society for comparison and contrast. To have a keener comprehension of a person, we might do well to consult the person's ex-spouse.

What, then, could furnish more accurate knowledge about art than its opposite, its antithesis, its enemy, its nonentity imitation, ART FORGERY?

Strangely enough, art forgery, the scourge of all that is proper, elegant, and beautiful in the art world, holds the key to the mystery that is art. For nothing exposes the fakery of the supposedly genuine article faster than the genuine article which turns out to be a fake. Hence it is the starting point in our search for the truth about collectible art.

Chapter 2

The Genuine Forgery

We all love genuine articles and hate forgeries. This cannot be more true than in the loftiest of all human endeavors—art. Only the most depraved and unconscionable of human beings, the consensus leaves no doubt on this, would ever produce fake artworks for personal gain, thereby dishonoring the masters and insulting the noble spirit of art lovers and collectors. For reasons that will become obvious, however, there have been and there are more art forgers than famous masters. These forgers have also become famous (or infamous) in their own right, primarily because of their exploits as forgers.

In recent memory three master forgers stand out as media celebrities and folk heroes. (A more complete listing of the activities of known forgers appears in Chapter Thirteen.)

Tom Keating of England "sexton blaked" (his term for forging) literally thousands of English and other masterworks, enough to rate a catalogue of his own. Celebrated and lionized in the media and in the book about him by Geraldine Norman, *The Fake's Progress*, he was completely at home with such famous artists as Degas, Renoir, Sisley, Rembrandt, Munch, and many more. On the wave of notoriety, not all of it negative, after his activities became known, he even appeared on BBC television, showing the viewer how forgeries are done.

Elmyr de Hory, the extraordinarily talented and prolific forger made famous by Clifford Irving in his book appropriately titled *Fake!* (and who himself later tried to write a Howard Hughes biography by faking interviews with the then-reclusive millionaire), sold to collectors and museums over two thousand forged paintings, supposedly by French Impressionists and post-Impressionists, in all different media. Doing it alone at first as a means of supporting himself while he tried to make it as an artist, he later teamed up with two partners who pushed his works in virtually every continent, one famous victim being the Texas oil millionaire, Algur Meadows. Pressured by Meadows' determined legal pursuit and weakened by its own internal squabbles, the team eventually broke up.

Perhaps the most famous of them all is the Dutch forger Han Van Meegeren. Although he produced only eight forgeries, an inconsequential number by prevailing standards, his eight Vermeers are undoubtedly history's most celebrated fakes. What made him a household name in the annals of art forgery and the very symbol of expert incompetence was the care with which he produced his first Vermeer, "Christ at Emmaus," which was the most talked-about painting at the time of its "discovery" in the thirties. Even *after* his confession and incontrovertible proof of forgery, the experts still argued among themselves and the event was stamped as one of the greatest triumphs of forgery over real art.

These are among the forgers who remain renowned because of their relatively recent exploits. But there are others no less prolific who are considered by art experts to be the standard bearers in the history of art forgery. Among them one would certainly name Alceo Dossena whose classical reproductions were as superb as they were varied in period and style; Otto Wacker, whose thirty-some Van Goghs were so good they had experts divided against each other over their authenticity, and in the case of one expert against himself; David Stein, whose talent was so great that he could produce a fake Picasso or Chagall almost while you waited.

Such celebrated art forgers as Keating and Stein, as well as many others of their calibre, are mentioned whenever art-people talk about forgery detection. We shall encounter them again and again in the following pages, for they, or rather their forgeries, bear silent or, sometimes, not so silent witness to the comedy and insanity of the art world. As celebrated as their names are and as widely publicized as their activities were, however, few of their forged paintings have ever been publicly recognized or destroyed. As Geraldine Norman observed in connection with Keating's sexton blakes, a forgery continues to circulate "until someone somewhere is gullible enough to believe it genuine and hang it on his wall as a master painting." In other words, forgeries make up a good proportion of the cultured business of art dealing, selling, buying, and collecting.

But what proportion? How many wolves in sheep's clothing mingle among the flock, masquerading as genuine, lovely sheep? How many forgeries are there in the art world that are being sold by dealers, bought by collectors, expounded on by experts, and admired by art lovers? Of course it is impossible to know, for the volume of art trade is nothing like the volume of the stockmarket. It is fairly secret and exclusive, and its total volume of trade (although reported to have topped a billion dollars in 1987) can only be estimated, since there is little strict record keeping for much of the business.

It is probably safe to assume that at least half of all artworks that are on public display and in private collections are forgeries. Many of them are courtesy of Keating, de Hory, Stein, and so on, but also of a horde of other forgers who have not been publicly exposed but who are just as productive. This figure of one-half, a fairly startling proportion to art lovers, is based on a variety of authoritative sources, which make it seem reasonably accurate. (Reasonable accuracy, given the peculiar nature of the art business, is perhaps all we can hope for.)

As sources of my estimate, take the following statements made by people with established credentials in the art world.

First, consider the statement made by a Sotheby's official, Peter Nahum, quoted in Ian Haywood's book, *Faking It* (p. 127): "*Forty per cent* of all goods on the [art] market to be 'wrong in some sense,' " "wrong" being a polite trade description for forgery. (Italics are my emphasis, to point out the essentially "conservative" estimate by such an established power-house art auctioneer as Sotheby's.)

Second, there is the observation made by Robert Wraight in his book, *The Art Game Again* (p. 84), that "breaking the news to the proud owners" (that their pictures are not genuine) "is a delicate task that staffs of the picture departments at Sotheby's, Christie's, and Parke-Bernet must perform dozens of times every day."

Third, Grace Glueck, reporting on the "clean up" job that the art world began in the 60s on art forgeries, in "The Expert's Guide to the Experts," *ARTnews*, November 1978, quotes one expert as estimating that "A complete reevaluation of the 600-odd Rembrandts in the world's inventory...will reduce the number to 350," and notes that the six Vermeers at the National Gallery of Art in Washington (not by Van Meegeren, of course) was reduced to three in the last few years, one of the remaining three still being suspected to be a forgery.

Fourth, in her book, *True or False? Amazing Art Forgeries*, Ann Waldron, lamenting on the proliferation of art forgeries (p. 17), quotes experts who told her that "Fakes outnumber the real thing."

There is a strong if unspoken consensus on the proliferation of forgeries circulating among the genuine ones, as casually described by the writers quoted above. None of the above quotations were made to discredit the art establishment, but were made out of concern for the prosperity of the art business. Those quoted all love art. They are part of the art world as scholars, collectors, or dealers, and as respected *participants* of the art market. None can be said to have an ax to grind against the art establishment. It is obvious that they are proud of collectible art and its traditional role in symbolizing the beautiful and the honorable as well as the profitable.

Their collective comments and observations therefore make my estimate of one-half fairly conservative. Its scientific accuracy may be disputed, but the fact that the art market itself *in general* accepts the figure as true should be good enough for those of us on the outside looking in. I have no personal knowledge of the extent of forgeries, having never dealt in the art business. Yet the literature on art forgery that I have examined with some interest seems to dovetail nicely and comfortably with the above experts' estimates. Plus or minus a few percentage points, to satisfy any contentious parties, would not make that much difference, either with the extent of art forgery or with the purpose we have in mind in discussing it as simple fact.

But why is this figure (of close to 50%) so important in our pursuit of truth? Why are we going through a painstaking construction of how many forgeries there may be among the artworks that are being sold and bought? Indeed, what's the point, other than our outsiders' delight at being able to say ha-ha to the embarrassed art-people who are so smug and arrogant with their expensive collections, that half of them are fakes?

Let me answer these questions and objections by raising the following question of my own: What if, strictly hypothetically speaking, *over or close to one-half of physicians and airline pilots were fakes*, people who are not real physicians or pilots passing for the genuine physicians and pilots? In this hypothesis, as an inevitable commonsense response to the profitable co-existence between fakes and reals, consider the *theoretical* possibility that every *other* brain surgeon, every *other* heart specialist, every *other* emergency room doctor, every *other* anesthesiologist, every *other* gynecologist, and so on, you may run into, could possibly be a fake. By the same token, so could every *other* pilot who flies jumbo jets, military fighter planes, hospital emergency helicopters, and what have you.

What if, indeed, such were the case?

(Let's, for the moment, suspend the argument as to the difference between art and medicine, and art and flying. We all know that they are different in nature and character, and hence cannot be compared with each other. It would be like comparing apples and oranges. While recognizing the differences between them, however, we can still insist on the categories of "real art" and "not-real art" that the *art establishment* itself insists on and in which it goes to a great length to emphasize the difference, as much as there is a difference between real medicine and not-real medicine, real flying and not-real flying, and so on. There must be something in real art to make it real, perhaps not as real as real medicine or flying, but real enough nevertheless in its own right, vis a vis forgeries, as art-people insist and we have no reason to reject their own distinction between real and not-real.)

Needless to say, the consequences of fake doctors and pilots, operating, dispensing medicine on people, and trying to fly 747s would be nothing short of catastrophic. Or, what if close to 50% of our money were bogus? Or, what if one-half of the air we breathe was fake air? Could the medical system, airline safety, the nation's economics, and the human body respectively survive more than a few days—or a few minutes in some case—with that many fakes passing as genuine?

Let's try to understand the phenomenon from the opposite end, to see if we could come to a better understanding of the puzzle. Let's assume that even with close to 50% of fake doctors and bogus pilots, *everything is fine*: Nobody dies of malpractice, no airplane crashes by pilot error. In other words, everything runs smoothly without a hitch year after year, decade after decade, or even century after century (that's how long forgeries have been in existence). In other words, fake doctors and real doctors, half and half, can operate as if *all* of them were *real* doctors, and fake pilots and real pilots as if real pilots, along side each other. Or, for that matter, one-half bogus money or one-half wrong air has absolutely no harmful effect in the economy or on the body respectively.

What could we conclude from this hypothesis? What sense indeed are we to make of this scenario? The only possible conclusion from this hypothesis, after all explanations have been properly considered, is that *there is nothing* to "real medicine," "real flying," "real money," or "real air." Why this conclusion? Because fake stuff worked just as well as real stuff, making absolutely no difference whether they were real or forged. Fake medicine and genuine medicine are the same; fake flying skill and trained flying skill are the same; bogus money and real money are the same; and real air and wrong air are the same. In this hypothetical follow-up, then, the only natural conclusion that we can logically draw and our commonsense can live with is that the "real" stuff is so "unreal" itself that it cannot be distinguished from the real "unreal."

From this conclusion, however, the problem is just beginning to take shape. If this is the case, then, how do we justify all that fuss we attach to "real" medicine, flying, money, or air? Why insist on the difference between real and unreal when there is absolutely no discernible difference? Why, if there is no obvious difference between forged and genuine, why would we condemn one and revere the other? Of course, these questions in the cases hypothesized above are moot, since we *do* make the distinctions between the two (real medicine vs. fake medicine, and so on) and the latter *cannot* pass for the former. The reason that the latter cannot is simply because we cannot possibly allow fakes to masquerade as real—not to the tune of one-half fakery.

Now let's get back to the subject of art and forgery.

We know for a fact that close to one-half of all known artworks in circulation—plus or minus a few percentage points—are forgeries passing for real ones. But there has been absolutely no chaos or collapse in the art world with repeated forgery scandals *and* with the extant volume of forgeries. If anything, the art business has multiplied in size and prospered in profit-making even with all the infusion of forgeries in its midst. So, what do we reasonably conclude from this harmony between real and unreal in the art world? Why has no catastrophe resulted from that much fakery in the art world which, in another field like medicine or flying, would have been a cosmic disaster immediate and terrible?

One possible answer we may consider would be that art isn't *that* important in personal life or in society. Therefore, this possibility concludes that, real or forged, it makes very little difference in the real world. What harm, we may ask, can a forged painting hung on the wall do, anyway? This conclusion, however, overlooks two very significant facts: One, the strenuous and concerted law-enforcement effort made by the art establishment to detect, expose, and get rid of forgeries; two, the enormous amount of money that is determined, say, between millions and a few dollars, by whether an artwork is considered real or forged. In either case when money gets involved, art-people's seriousness cannot be doubted. If something is so *un*important in life so as to allow one-half of itself to be filled by fakery without *any* detrimental effect, society would not possibly tolerate its existence, much less as the object of such admiration and possession. Of course, that is, unless...

From this simple fact we can fathom drawing no other conclusion except simply: FORGED ART AND GENUINE ART ARE THE SAME. Or, to put it another way, forgeries can *replace* real stuff without any harm. The history of art collection proves that this is so. What else are we to think, given the facts and their logical implications?

But the real problem begins precisely here: What in the world does that *mean*? If forgeries can exist side by side with genuine stuff and absolutely nothing happens as a result, how "genuine" is the "genuine stuff"? How can we possibly insist on real art and condemn forgeries when their half-and-half coexistence makes absolutely no difference?

Let's consider the sentence left unfinished above: Something half-real and half-unreal is not only tolerated but is also the object of unusual admiration and possessive desire. How is this contradiction possible?

The established art world could suggest, as a way out of this dilemma, that the percentage of forgeries is not really as high as that. Let's say that the art establishment insists that it is much lower than that, say, 40% or 30% or 20%. If this were true, although highly unlikely (in fact

50% is a conservative estimate), it might *weaken* the argument, weaken as much as the decline in the percentage point, but not wholly *negate* it. I would argue, rather, that even 20% of fakery among real stuff, with no harmful effect, casts a grave doubt on the "realness" of the real stuff which allows that proportion of fakery to be mixed with itself without visible detection or functional harm.

The dilemma is now obvious. If art is to be taken as real, as art-people claim it is, then forgery must be accepted as real also, as it makes up one-half of "real art" in circulation. If forgery is thus accepted as real—and here is the crux of the dilemma—then "real art" can no longer claim to be real, for no longer can it be real when one-half of its realness consists of forgery, which is not real.

There is, however, one possibility we have not so far considered as a way out of this dilemma, for it indeed is a dilemma for the art establishment. If it insists that there is a difference between real art and unreal art, then it must explain the existence of the one-half of forgeries in its midst. Failing to explain this, it places itself in a dilemma of having to admit that its own "realness" is not so real after all, not any more real than the forgeries it condemns. What is the one route from which to escape this dilemma? It is in the argument that the so-called "experts" called on to authenticate artworks are *incompetents* who botch up their job for *half of the time* they are asked to determine the "attribution" (authorship) of an artwork.

The thought that experts as a whole can botch up their jobs one out of every two times they are called upon to exercise their expertise is fairly mind-boggling in itself. And while this may be a plausible thought to consider as a theoretical possibility, which is the art world's standard line of defense in having to explain its dilemma, the incompetent-expert factor has its own host of problems to defend and explain away.

This we will consider next.

Chapter 3

The Experts' Dilemmas

It inevitably happens that every art controversy is at once an art scandal and a spectacle of experts, the latter contradicting themselves and one another, and pronouncing art's authenticity or inauthenticity often on grounds entirely unrelated to art. Doing so with each scandal, the experts peel off another layer in the honor and mystery of art.

This spectacle of experts comes in a variety of ways. Before we can discuss the "problem" of expertise in art, namely, their incompetence, we ought to look at some prominent examples that abound in art stories. These stories are so standard in the art world as to require no specific reference for their sources.

ITEM: An expert first swears that Artwork X by, say, Van Gogh, is "really" by Van Gogh. A little while later, however, the expert changes his mind and says that Artwork X is really a forgery. Then the expert changes his mind once again and says he was originally right: Artwork X *was* by Van Gogh. This actually happened with Otto Wacker's "Van Goghs," in the late 20s in Germany, which had suddenly materialized in Wacker's gallery under rather mysterious circumstances. The explanation given by Wacker was that the paintings had come into his hands from a Russian nobleman whose name or court appearance could not be produced even upon legal prodding. At any rate, a famous Van Gogh expert (his name is not important) blessed the 30 new Van Goghs as genuine and thus included them in his newly-compiled Van Gogh catalogue. A year later, upon learning that some of the paintings had been turned down for a Dutch exhibition of Van Goghs, the expert changed his mind and decided that all 30 were forgeries. As the controversy over the authenticity of Wacker's Van Goghs erupted, the expert, three years later, changed his mind once again and declared that at least "some" of them—seven to be exact—were genuine Van Goghs, an opinion he held until his death.

ITEM: This flip-flop can also occur with the same artwork, not with the same expert. An artwork is initially accepted as real, then is declared a forgery, and then, some time later, is reclaimed as real. This happened at the prestigious Metropolitan Museum of Art in New York.

A small bronze Greek horse, "one of the Metropolitan's prized possessions—considered to be 2,400 years old," was purchased in 1923. For close to 45 years the artwork was praised from every art-loving quarter as the "most beautiful 5th century, B.C. Greek horse," adorning every handsomely illustrated art book and highlighting every literature put out by the Met for publicity. Then in 1967, it was suddenly declared a modern forgery because of the way it was put together, a technique considered nonexistent in Greece at the time. The bronze horse promptly vanished from its accustomed place of glory at the museum. Ten years or so later, however, a more powerful X-ray penetration technique had been developed, which showed, that the Greek horse *was* indeed a genuine work of art, upon which the horse, now corroborated by other archaeological evidence then available, reclaimed its place of honor at the Met and became the "most beautiful 5th century B.C. Greek horse" again where it still remains so—perhaps until the next pronouncement.

ITEM: A variation on the above item is an expert who insists upon the artwork being "real" even *after* the forger's confession and scientific evidence of its forgery. In one of the most bizarre and celebrated cases of forgery, soon after World War II, Dutch forger Han Van Meegeren found himself charged with the crime of collaborating with the hated-Nazis when authorities traced a Vermeer in Reichsmarschall Hermann Goering's possession to him as the original seller, still not suspecting forgery. After wavering between the penalty for collaboration with the enemy—possibly death—and for forging a signature—much lighter penalty—Van Meegeren confessed to having forged seven Vermeers, one of which ended up in the Reichsmarschall's collections. Disbelieving, the experts demanded proof. Van Meegeren obliged, by painstakingly reconstructing all the steps he had taken to insure the creation of a perfect forgery and, as an added measure, actually painting an 8th Vermeer in full view of experts and jail guards. A scientific committee also examined the paintings and confirmed the forger's confession. But even after all this evidence, which established the Vermeers as Van Meegeren's beyond any reasonable doubt, some experts held out to the bitter end that the paintings (at least two of them) *were* real Vermeers, never mind the forger's confession, his actual demonstration, and the scientific corroboration. One expert even boasted that "If Van Meegeren is the author [of the Vermeers], I'll eat my hat." The expert didn't have to, because he died with the matter still in dispute. The Dutch court wasn't sure either and made an exception to the rule of destroying all evidence determined to be forgeries, by ordering the "Vermeers" preserved—just in case they were real. The experts who believed them to be real Vermeers never relented from their conviction.

ITEM: Even the most exhaustive application of all known scientific methods can fail miserably in telling real art from a forgery. Van Meegeren's first, and admittedly his best, forgery ("Christ at Emmaus") was appraised by an expert who had applied all known measures to insure its authenticity. The five major applications of scientific detection on art forgery at the time were: (1) looking at the picture by a well-trained eye, also called "connoisseurship"; (2) subjecting the paints to alcohol and other solvents for authentic "age"; (3) evidence of white lead in the white portions, also for age; (4) X-ray penetration to see what's underneath the picture to make sure the picture was not painted over another; and (5) microscopic examination of pigments to detect any modern materials. The famous expert—now made infamous by this mistake—, after three days of rigorous examination, praised the painting thusly in part: "It is a wonderful moment in the life of a lover of art when he finds himself suddenly confronted with a hitherto unknown painting by a great master... *the* masterpiece of Johannes Vermeer...In no other picture by the great Master of Delft do we find such sentiment, such a profound understanding of the Bible story—a sentiment so nobly expressed through the medium of the highest art." (Italics are original.) A string of other experts, following suit one after another, also gave their individual blessings to "Emmaus." The painting hung at the museum as the centerpiece of the Queen's Fortieth Jubilee celebration and for many years thereafter.

ITEM: Then, the error of expertise is not confined to the cases of individual experts making isolated errors alone. It happens also, "collectively," to a *committee* of experts, which, again, involves Han Van Meergren's forgery. One of his admittedly inferior Vermeers was sold to the Dutch state museum after passing the inspection by a government committee made up of prominent experts, which advised purchase of the painting. One of the experts on the committee, director of a large museum, in particular confessed during Van Meegeren's forgery trial that "None of us [on the committee] liked [the painting] very much," but decided to purchase it anyway because Vermeers were "scarce," eventually paying a huge sum for the forgery. When asked about it during the trial, the red-faced experts blamed their blunder on "war time patriotism," by saying that if they hadn't recommended its purchase the Vermeer would have fallen into the hands of the Germans, their hated enemies during World War II.

ITEM: The most common of all spectacles is that of experts disagreeing among themselves over particular paintings, one side arguing they are real and the other saying they are forgeries. Experts on the staff of an auction house often lock horns with those of another auction house, Sotheby's versus Agnew's, for example, most commonly over a painting whose genuineness or forgery could multiply or obliterate its market value. Sometimes an expert says Artwork X is real until he is told of another expert's opinion which says it is forged, upon which the former reconsiders his opinion and soon changes his mind, agreeing with the latter. At other times, nationalities of experts matter a great deal, often pitting one nationality—say, British—against another—say, German—in which case national feelings more than art authenticity are at stake. Most often, however, it is strictly a matter of personal opinion. During Tom Keating's trial two experts offered diametrically opposing opinions on the quality of Keating's workmanship: One said it was "an appalling little piece of rubbish," while the other (even knowing the works were forgeries) said they "still have the same effect" on him. The most famous case involves the Wacker-Van Goghs in which experts lined up on *both* sides of the issue, while one expert (mentioned earlier) flip-flopped between them, making them all angry with him. This division of opinion continued even after the considerable evidence that Wacker's Van Goghs might be forgeries. But of course, in the case of Van Meegeren's Vermeers, some experts insisted that they were real even after the forger had already signed a confession.

ITEM: If experts are so incompetent and inconsistent, can artists themselves tell their *own* works? Sometimes not. All artists are critics themselves in many ways, often their own best critics. It is said that they are the best judge of their own workmanship. But how good are they as critics of their *own* works? Well, as it turns out, not very good, especially if they happen to be as prolific as someone like Picasso. It is widely known that Picasso couldn't tell whether his own works— or works bearing his signature—were indeed *his own* or not. Stories abound that tell of how he had to ask about the price of the artwork in question to see if it could have been his own. If the price paid for it was high enough, he was inclined to believe it was his. Elmyr de Hory tells the story of how he and his accomplices fooled a well-known artist, slightly advanced in age (van Dongen), to sign his name on a de Hory forgery. Also another part of the de Hory saga is about how experts pronounced the real works by the artist under consideration as forgeries, while authenticating de Hory's forgeries of the same artist as "real."

ITEM: Finally, lavish praise from experts is often a death knell for artists, especially if this praise happens to have been heaped on fake artworks. The more lavish the original praise by some of the experts the greater the criticism shown by other critics once the fakery is exposed, as if the entire expert community is making up for its own follies with vengeance. Works once praised to no end, such as those by Van Meegeren, tend to be savagely attacked when the table is turned. In 1951 an artist in Germany was contracted to restore the frescoes in a medieval church (another well known story). But, unable to find the original frescoes on the wall to restore once the protective varnish had been removed, and afraid of false accusations for having destroyed the original, the talented forger faked the entire frescoes himself. They were then praised—of course, in the name of the original medieval artist—as "brilliant," "celestial," and "entirely unique...to be found nowhere else in the world." When the artist confessed to his fakery a year later after a falling-out with the contractor over money, they put him in jail for eighteen months. His crime: Having created brilliant, celestial, and entirely unique frescoes to be found nowhere else in the world. If his praise hadn't been so lavish in the first place, we may surmise, punishment for his "crime" might not have been so severely meted out. Alceo Dossena, another talented forger, whose fake bust of a famous Florentine poet and philosopher was "worshipped" as a "masterpiece" of "amazing vitality," also suffered humiliation when his forgeries came to light (also having had a falling-out with his middleman over money); he died in a paupers' hospital in Rome.

Having considered some outstanding examples of the experts' follies from these sketches, what are we now to make of them?

The most immediate response, hence the most standard explanation, is that the experts are plainly *incompetent* with their function of art authentication. How else could we account for the display of such contradictory and inconsistent expert behavior? This response, that the experts—at least some of them—are incompetent, is of course the standard one issued by the art establishment whenever the question of art authenticity arises. This is how the art world responds in its conventional way: Yes, there are some incompetent experts. Yes, there are also competent experts in the art world. Yes, art buyers must be careful in choosing experts when they are contemplating art purchases. Yes, there is a directory of art experts available at any art dealership and art gallery. Yes, above all, art expertise, like all other expertises, is not fool-proof; mistakes and errors do occur; we are sorry but such mistakes and errors are all part of this very delicate business known as art, etc., etc.

However, we instinctively suspect that something is not right with this standard response. Even if this incompetence factor, the art world's last line of defense, is accepted at its face value it requires some further clarification.

For one thing, how do we explain the fact, as seen in some of the examples cited above, that even world-renown, highly competent experts whose authority is beyond reproach *still* are divided among *themselves*. Not infrequently, these experts were also contradicting themselves, flip-flopping several times over the authenticity of the same artworks. We might say that experts in *other fields*, even highly technical and scientific ones such as astronomy and economics, are divided along partisan lines, and the art experts are no different. But this apology doesn't hold water in view of the simple fact that experts in astronomy and economics do not have all the necessary facts before them—after all, stars are far away and consumers haven't decided how to spend their money yet—whereas art experts have *everything* they need right in front of them: Namely, the artwork under consideration.

For another, the art world must explain why the experts fail *so often*. In fact the experts fail so frequently in their tasks that the ratio of successful expertise to failed expertise is no better than the ratio of heads to tails when a coin is flipped randomly. As often as they fail, one out of every two cases, we might as well *not* consult experts or have expertise at all in art. Just going by *chance* would result in the same success-failure ratio, or possibly better, since flipping the coin logically results in half-heads and half-tails. Why have the experts at all when they are no better than the probability resulting from sheer luck or chance?

We might console ourselves, I suppose, by being more understanding of and more charitable toward their dilemma, that without the art experts the ratio of forgeries to real art would be *much higher* in favor of the former than the present ratio of 50:50. While this consolation may sound reasonable for the experts, its implications are nothing less than catastrophic for art itself. For this would imply that we should allow forgeries to continue to exist at the "tolerable" level of 50%, thanks to experts and their expertise! But can a field of human endeavor that is sophisticated enough to claim expertise tolerate this failure rate and still claim expertise?

The catastrophic dimension of the art experts' follies, hence the unacceptability of the incompetence-factor, becomes clearer if we superimposed art expertise upon medical expertise for comparison. Suppose a medical doctor is called in to tell whether the body under consideration is a real human body or one that is actually a robot that passes for a real one. First, after some considerable examination, he pronounces the body a real one. But, then, he reconsiders the case for a while and says the body is actually a robot. Soon, he changes his mind once again, apologizing profusely for the error, and says the body is definitely real. Fairly dissatisfied and confused, the client calls in a *group* of medical experts to settle the issue. Now we know the rest of the story: The group of experts, all authorities in their fields, at once proceed to quarrel among themselves over the body, some saying it is real and some saying it is robotic. Is it conceivable, under this improbable scenario, that either (1) the client would ever trust the so-called medical experts again, or (2) the so-called medical experts should ever claim their authoritative expertise again?

In defense of art and art expertise we might be inclined to say that the two cases are different from each other and thus ought not be compared. Granted, they are different. But *in what ways* are they different? If we say the body and the artwork are not the same, there will be no argument. Surely they are two different things. But if we said medical expertise and art expertise *as expertises* are different, for example, that experts in one field are *more expert* than those in the other, then we should immediately take issue with that statement. For medical expertise and art expertise *as expertise* are not one bit different. Both are expertises in their respective fields as long as the term is applicable in both cases. Medical expertise should be able to tell a real human body from a robot because such competence is expected of its experts.

Art expertise, on the other hand, should be able to tell what is art and what is not in the ratio of success that approaches the success ratio in medical expertise, for we have no reason to believe that one expertise should be any less of expertise than another in their most fundamental tasks. To use another example, we would expect diamond experts to be able to tell real diamonds from fake ones practically all of the time they are put to the test. When an art expert pronounces that an artwork under consideration is a genuine Van Gogh, should we trust his pronouncement to the same degree that we would trust a doctor's diagnosis on a real human body and a diamond expert's certification on a real diamond? Of course, not. But why not?

Indeed, it is the crux of the whole matter: Why is it *not* the case with art expertise? The simple and easy reference to expert incompetence explains nothing of the dilemma that the art establishment has put itself in in view of the staggering number of expert failures as seen above.

Considering all these problems intrinsic to art expertise, as we have seen so far, the standard response from the art world of the incompetence factor ignores one crucial but fairly simple fact: That the very *nature* of art expertise is nothing like that in any other field of expertise. And very possibly, it is *not* even an expertise. Then, what makes art expertise so different from all of the others and possibly nonexistent? Why is the art world's incompetence factor so irrelevant as an explanation for the failures?

As the mystery gradually unfolds, we will come fact to face with a strange fact: It is *art*, not art experts or their competence, that makes art expertise so different from anything else and so irrelevant as a reasonable explanation for its appalling failures.

But, first things first.

Chapter 4

The "Un-expertisable" Art of Art Expertise

Of all expertises, art expertise is unique simply because there is no standard way of getting it. One does not go to school or complete a pre-established series of courses to become an art expert. Although a college education helps, it is not essential. Many become art experts simply as a family trade, father to son, son to grandson. This fact makes it both easy and difficult to become an art expert. It is easy to become one because all one has to do is to declare himself an art expert since it requires neither a certificate nor a particular set of qualifications. But what makes it so easy in theory is also, and most significantly, what makes it so difficult to be an art expert in practice. While anyone can declare himself an art expert, not anyone who so declares can *practice* as an art expert. Here is the crux of the matter: Art is perhaps the *only* area in which an expert's *whole lifetime's* reputation is needed to qualify him as an art expert.

Unlike medical expertise or astronomic expertise, or any other technical fields of expertise for that matter, art expertise has no such objective, specific criteria by which its experts are certified. No minimum education is required for it; yet no maximum formal education would necessarily qualify one for it. This simple fact puts enormous pressure on the factor of "reputation" as one single criterion that has to be tested and proven time and time again in *actual practice*. But as we all know, reputation is the most difficult commodity to acquire, and hence the best way to get to know who is the highest authority in any field.

Consider the fact that reputation cannot be obtained by advertising it, by bragging about one's superiority, or by aggressively going after it. It has to *come* to the person, not the other way around. Even in France where the expert is certified by the government, this certification has more to do with one's established reputation than with any academic or prescribed procedure for qualification. There are many college graduates in fine arts, art history, museology, archaeology, and what have you in the United States as well as in Europe, but the academic pedigree has little or nothing to do with their establishment as art experts.

Art expertise is one of those rare trades, as noted, that are often handed down generation to generation. Many of the world's leading authorities on art hail from the recognized family trees of art experts, going back for many generations. Often one starts out as an apprentice at the bottom of the art world and, as one gathers one's experience and knowledge, he slowly moves up the ladder of recognition by others in the art community. Finally, his established reputation is such that he can stand on his own as an "expert," meaning that such recognition is sufficient enough for him to use the expertise as the chief means of his economic survival, and possibly prosperity as well.

Understandably, of course, in view of this unspecified ways of art expertise, there are some shoddy individuals who take advantage of this loose or nonexistent criteria for expertization and declare themselves knowledgeable about art business and offer their services to unsuspecting customers. It is not uncommon that at the lower end of the art world pyramid there is a considerable number of such individuals who, with only marginal expertise or knowledge, survive on the fringes of respectability with their cunning and wits. They may move from one cheap country auction to another, buying, selling, and otherwise dealing in large quantities of cheap goods, mostly aiming for the low-budget echelons of art business. But, as numerous as these individuals may be, they are almost *never* called into service when high-stake pictures become the issue. None of these fringe characters would ever dream of being involved, especially as expert witnesses or authorities, in cases as illustrious as Van Meegeren, Wacker, Keating, or other such famous disputes. In each of these cases, only the most reputable, the most-established, and the very best authorities and experts were brought into service. In general practice, large individual collectors and public museums only call on such recognized experts whose reputation is beyond question.

It is clear then that there is no fly-by-night art expertise, especially in the upper echelons of art business where stakes are high and publicity is worldwide. When a dispute must be settled in a court of law, therefore, we can expect nothing but the highest and most honorable representation of expert competence in the field.

In fact, as expertise goes, I would argue that becoming an art expert is, if not the most difficult one, certainly one of the most difficult social processes in status-attainment simply because it is based on reputation and virtually nothing else. Time and time again, year after year, during one's whole lifetime, one must prove oneself worthy of that honorific title of "art expert." No college degree, no quick snow job, no simple technical training will help, at least not in any significantly lasting way. Of all the fields of human endeavor where a measure of expertise can be claimed, therefore, I would put art expertise at the very top for the difficulty of attaining and maintaining it. If these art experts had chosen another field and devoted their lifetime to its technical mastery, their expertise would have been almost *infallible*. Obviously such peculiarities in the way art expertise is established and practiced put further strain on the incompetence factor as an explanation for the proliferation of forgeries.

(Robert Wraight suggests, somewhat against the incompetence theory, what amounts to a "corruption" theory. He says as an alternate explanation, that it is the pressure from dealers as well as the personal relationships that the expert may develop in the course of his business that is responsible for the tendency to be deliberately "positive" toward forgeries and bad art, pronouncing them real art even when there is an element of doubt. While true to some extent, it does not explain everything, for this kind of financial and personal pressure is not altogether unique to the art world. Wherever there is need for authoritative interpretations, we might say, such sources of pressure do exist and work on the expert's conscience virtually in any field.)

After all pertinent factors have been duly recognized and considered thusly, however, the puzzle remains yet unanswered: *Why do the experts, with all their expertise that takes a lifetime to be established and honored, still fail to perform the simple task for which they are supremely qualified, telling real art and fake art apart one-half of the time they are called to perform it?*

What's wrong with these so-called experts? What indeed is wrong with them?

Our answer must be, since there is nothing wrong with the expertise itself: *Nothing*, absolutely nothing is wrong with either the experts or their expertise.

Then, what *accounts* for their miserable failure rate?

Expert incompetence is a nice, easy answer. So is the corruption theory. But neither answer applies when persons of impeccable credentials and highest reputations stumble time and time again. On the other hand, if this "incompetence" or "corruption" were so widespread as to constitute one-half of its legitimate business, why, it would make the very notion of expertise a laughing stock. Such being obviously untrue, then it is *not* their expertise that should be called to question. But then, what, if not expert incompetence or corruption to explain it?

What's wrong is neither the expert nor his expertise. It is *what the expert is trying to be expert in, which is wrong*: Namely, ART ITSELF.

To state the issue in the most succinct manner possible: ART CANNOT BE "EXPERTISABLE!" It is *"un*expertisable," to coin a new but entirely appropriate word.

One can be an expert in medicine, in astronomy, or in diamond cutting, but *not in art*, because art is not something that allows itself to be expertised. No matter how long one studies art, how competent one becomes in understanding it, how exalted one's reputation is in it, it is all for naught. No one can ever be an expert in art simply because art is not something in which one can attain expertise.

But this conclusion is incredulous, if not ridiculous. It goes against everything we know about art. It is like saying the earth is flat. How is this possible? the question is immediately raised. But our answer is, how can it be *otherwise*?

As we look closer we see two parts to the answer given above. The first is logical, the second historical—or "empirical" as social scientists would say—, the latter making the former inevitable.

Let's consider the logical impossibility of thinking otherwise. As we have painstakingly constructed above, how else can we explain the simple fact that (1) experts of the highest reputation and knowledge are called into task when art authentication is the issue and no one else can do a better job; and (2) they fail as often as they succeed with their task, which stands no better than the probability of chance or luck, or expertise offered by a man-in-the-street?

Let's now consider the historical fact that bears upon the logical answer given above. There is no way we can avoid the simple fact that art *is* so *easy* to *copy*. Classic masterworks—as shown in Van Meegeren's Vermeers—can be copied rather easily if the forger is technically competent and patient enough to pull it off. The techniques developed by modern science to detect forgeries are also known to the forger and, if he is determined enough, the forger can fool experts rather handily using their own knowledge, as Van Meegeren had done. Expertise is made absolutely helpless, becoming the subject of public ridicule and scorn time and time again, in the face of this simple fact that the technical demand for classic forgeries can easily be met.

Modern collectibles, which are increasingly the target of contemporary forgeries, are much easier than classics to forge as shown in the thousands of fakes that de Hory made of Picasso, Matisse, Modigliani, and others. As collectible art has shifted from classics to moderns, the emphasis of the artist's technical perfection has also shifted to the emphasis of the artist's "ideas" to be embodied in the work. But unlike in uncollectible art forms (such as literature, music, film, philosophy), the so-called ideas expressed by modern artists are relatively obscure and metaphoric, and fairly nonexistent if the medium happens to be Conceptual Art or Minimalism, or something similar in style. This fact makes the modern collectibles fair game for forgery. It is relatively easy to copy what is basically obscure, metaphoric, and often nonexistent. Who but the most extremely untalented, helpless children, and the totally unimaginative would find Jo Baer's empty canvas impossible to copy? Only the most audacious or deceptive among us would argue that experts can tell a pencil drawing by Matisse from a pencil drawing by a talented forger, or an empty canvass by Jo Baer from one made by an average forger.

Let's look more closely at the basic elements of expertise. In order for one to become an expert in some field, all things being equal, two elements are necessary: First, the *person* must be competent enough to master the required expertise; and second, the *field*, in which the expertise is sought, must be such that it is an "expertisable" field. When the first criterion is present beyond doubt, as in the lifetime devotion of the person in mastering the expertise, yet his expertise fails him as miserably as if he wholly lacked his expertise, then the only conclusion possible is that the *second criterion* hasn't been met.

What is an expertisable field? An expertisable field must be (1) a definite subject, which is (2) systematically structured in such a way (3) that its substance can be unraveled by a step-by-step method of inquiry. Medicine is expertisable; so is astronomy; so is diamond-cutting. But "dream analysis" is not expertisable; nor is witchcraft; nor is *art*.

Art expertise is simply impossible to attain, not because of any defects in the expert, but because of the intrinsic nature of art itself. Every critic of forged art claims to defend true art from imposters, but he cannot tell actually *which* ones to defend and *which* ones to condemn, his noble intentions notwithstanding. He sometimes condemns true art, sometimes worships forgeries, sometimes flip-flops between the two over the same piece of art. And he is the most authoritative of experts in the field. But, as we have seen, it is not his fault, but the fault of the subject matter which is *believed, thought,* and *claimed* to be expertisable, but *delivered* only half the time. Hence the problem and confusion.

Not only is art un-expertisable. Its un-expertisableness brings no particular pain to this world. The expert's inability to tell real art from faked art, and their side-by-side coexistence, have no ill consequences whatsoever, neither for the seller who sells a forgery, nor for the buyer who buys it for a real one, nor for the viewer of the fakery, since it makes no difference in art *whether it is real or forged.* The expert is criticized, not for praising a forgery, but for changing his opinion of the same work *after* the hoax has been discovered, thus causing great discomfort and inconvenience for a lot of people, which many a so-called expert has done. If the hoax had remained undiscovered—as in the case of Van Meegeren's Vermeers—such forgeries would have still retained the expert's profound admiration. Once the signature on the collectible is believed to be true, then the expert sees everything that is beautiful, wonderful, and creative in it. Once the name is believed to be "wrong" on the other hand, the expert sees everything that is ugly, imperfect, and imitative. The moral of this is simple enough for us: One sees what one *wants* to see.

If these experts had the mind to examine the absurdity and illogic of their "expertise" when these contradictions occur, they would easily discover that the absurdity and illogic are in the field of art itself, not in their own expertise. But a lifetime is too long a time to acquire and consolidate a belief, especially when one earns a living with it, to discard upon reflection only because reflection is forced upon them by the force of absurdity and illogic.

Even when, at least in the *other* 50% of the cases, the authenticity of a collectible is established as beyond doubt, the lot of art and art experts does not improve much. What does it really mean, to say that Artwork X is *beyond a doubt* by Michelangelo? Is it Michelangelo's artistic beauty that has been established beyond a doubt? Or, is it the fact that Artwork X is beyond a doubt *by* Michelangelo, regardless of its artistic beauty? Which is being established? The artistic beauty or the *authorship*? Is *everything* by Michelangelo of artistic beauty? Is it the beauty of the artwork that is established? Then, why try so hard to establish whether it is *by* Michelangelo? The dilemma continues.

First, if artistic beauty is the main point to be established why is the authorship so important? Why do experts argue over whether Artwork X is by Artist Y, rather than whether X is of sufficient artistic beauty or not? Second, if authorship is the prime concern—as it is in practical business reality—why pretend to be involved in artistic judgment when the real concern is authorship, and subsequently its market value? The first question of artistic beauty makes the second one of authorship irrelevant, for the question is if it is beautiful art, not by whom. The second question of authorship makes the first one of artistic beauty irrelevant, for all we care to know is if it was *done* by that famous painter, not how artistic it is.

Of considerable theoretical importance, especially to those who like consistency in human thinking, is another related problem. That is, if only "experts" can tell if Artwork X is real art or fakery, then X can no longer be an "artwork." It will then simply be a *thing* like a diamond or a medical license. The question here has to be whether the diamond is a real diamond, or the medical license is a real medical license, not whether we "like" it or not as we do with art. Art is like love, the lover has to "feel" it to decide if it is love or not. No one would ever ask a doctor or a scientist, or any other "expert," to tell him if his love for Person X is real or not. He can legitimately ask the expert, of course, if his temperature indicates real pneumonia or not. But if he has to ask the art expert if Artwork X is real art done by Artist Y, then his is not a question of art, but a simple technical matter of identity. Expertise is brought in to determine if X is real only if X is a *thing*, a material object, not an artwork.

In many ways, the increasing involvement of "scientific" machines and techniques in art authentication, hailed by some as the new savior in art expertise, only makes art irrelevant and certainly proves my point. For these machines and techniques can only see material *things*, not artworks. Thus, authenticity may be established by expertise, but art must be lost in the process because it is no longer relevant to the technical matter of identifying a material object—like a diamond or a corpse. On the other hand, art may be established by our own aesthetic judgment about it, but expertise must be lost in the process because it is no longer relevant to our feeling and judgment (like love). Either way, this problem only pushes the dilemma deeper into the hole.

The dilemma invites yet another strange fact about art expertise. Everyone can "see" a picture hung on the wall, such as the "empty canvas" I saw at the modern art exhibition, but it is "invisible" to one— that is, until the expert makes it "visible" with his expertise. I "saw" the empty canvas, but I might as well have seen an "invisible" picture, for I was getting "nothing" from what I was seeing. That is, until I read the expert's description posted next to it. By writing the description, as quoted earlier, the expert helped me now "see" a "luminescent shadow rather than a direct contrast," "an almost imperceptible tension," and a "space and a window" in the painting that had been totally invisible to me without it. With his magic wand, the expert made the invisible picture visible for me, which happens all the time in the art world. But is this necessarily a blessing for the art expert or for art?

I think not, both for the art expert and for art. For the art expert, this magic function makes him extremely gullible to his own imaginations and nonsensical "expertise," for anything he says seems to matter little or none as far as reality is concerned. Since the public can see nothing in it, *anything* the expert says to make it a *something* is the only thing available about art and therefore, if one is interested in further understanding of art, must be accepted and appreciated. This fact can make the expert easily impressed with himself, pompously arrogant with his own power of expertise, and, worst of all, carelessly inventive with his interpretations. It is only natural that if one has the sole possession of magical power, one is likely to subject oneself to less than strenuous processes of self-control and discipline. And, ultimately, to irrelevance.

For art itself, this fact also bodes ill. An invisible artwork, whose visibility can be attained only by the expert, is an easy mark for copy-cats. It is so intangible as a material object that anyone can create it as well as duplicate it without much trouble. If a diamond expert mistook glass for diamond every other time he looks at one, he would surely be out of business in no time. Why doesn't the same thing happen to the art expert? If art is invisible to our naked eyes without the expert's help, then it simply means collectible art can be *anything* to qualify as art. As in the case of the empty canvas, even a nothing can be something in art. That being the case, why would a mistake of seeing something in a nothing be of any consequence? Where there is no concrete existence in art, for no-art is just as much art as real-art, it cannot possibly be expertisable. Where a nothing can be art, which materializes when an expert makes it so, the distinction between what is real and not real is necessarily made impossible.

If collectible art is really an invisible nothing, materializing miraculously only by the magic wand of experts, and there is no real difference between true art and faked art, it is clear that this "unintelligibility" (or "nothing-ness") of art is the result of its "un-expertisability." Then, how do we explain the undeniable fact that this nothing-ness has become a billion dollar business, which is nothing short of a miracle?

Here is the crucial role of art experts who, by their seemingly magical powers, transform nothing into something, invisibility into concreteness, so little into so much. For in collectible art, expertise is everything that art is.

How and why?

Chapter 5

The Public Not Invited

In collectible art, especially modern collectibles, as we have seen, it is the expert that makes something an artwork. The expert is the pillar that buttresses the whole phantom phenomenon of art, and it is his pronouncements that make the very notion of art possible. The expert gives meaning to the hitherto meaningless, renders visible what is hitherto invisible, and transforms into something what is hitherto nothing. In fact, art's dependence on experts is so complete that it is reasonable to say that the expert *is* art.

On the other hand, an expert in the uncollectible fields of literature, music, film, drama, and so on, while "hang[ing] on desperately in each field," as Tom Wolfe has observed in *The Painted Word*, has little or nothing to do with the life, death, and existence of uncollectible art. "The public that buys books in hardcover and paperback by the millions," to quote him further, "the public that buys records by the billions and fills stadiums for concerts, the public that spends $100 million in a single movie—this public affects taste, theory, and artistic outlook in literature, music, and drama... *The same has never been true in (collectible) art.*" (Italics and word in parenthesis supplied.)

The situation of expertise-dependence is entirely unique to collectible art. It is absent in any other field, be it science, law, psychology, or any such human endeavor. It is also absent in its sister art forms, namely uncollectible art, in that the public remains wholly uninvited to judge a phenomenon as common as art. An average person of average intelligence and education can say *something* about matters scientific, legalistic, psychology-related and, even more so as Tom Wolfe has observed, in areas of books, music, drama. The average person expects to actually participate even with only cursory knowledge in the subject, especially in the latter areas of art, as a concert-goer, a book-reader, a play-watcher, or simply as an arm-chair critic of this artwork or that. Most uncollectible artworks—books, plays, recordings, film—sustain their existence, or die out as art, entirely depending on the public's direct affection or lack of it. No matter what the expert says, it is the public, through its purchase of copies and attendance of performances, that has the final say about the artistic merit of this or that work. Most uncollectible artists—writers, composers, film-makers, dramatists—regardless of their artistic messages or egos, are acutely aware of this long shadow of the public when they engage in their creative activity. If people flock to see "Romeo and Juliet" it's not because it is by Shakespeare or because an expert has said it is a good play to see but because people "like" the story and "approve" it. Art critic Konstantin Bazarov in his essay "Emperors with no Clothes" similarly observes that in music "Far more people are prepared to trust their own responses" than be told what they like.

But almost never is this the case with collectible, especially modern collectible art. The public remains almost wholly ignorant and is therefore wholly dependent on the oracles of expert opinion. Why is the public totally nonexistent as a force in the world of collectible art? The reason, as we have seen, is already clear. But it needs to be reiterated: Collectible art *itself* is nonexistent, materializing only when the expert gives his magical blessings that are wholly incomprehensible and mysterious to the lay public. We may say that Artwork X looks "strange," "shocking," "colorful," or any number of such elementary things about it, but it is only the expert that gives—or, depending on his inclination, withholds from—it its final legitimacy. This process properly keeps us in awe of the expert. How could he get that (or that *much*) out of *so* little, or such significance out of such insignificance, or such clarity out of such chaos? we can only wonder. If an art expert says a stick of wood, appropriately framed, is a great work of art we have no other choice but *accept* his word for it. We know nothing and we are expected to know nothing, and, most important of all, there is *nothing* to know about it.

If a psychiatrist says Person X is crazy we can at least "see" some of his behavior that confirms the pronouncement or, failing to see anything wrong with the man's behavior, we can criticize the psychiatrist's diagnosis as wrong, all in a perfectly reasonable manner. Psychiatry, while a fairly esoteric profession with its own nonsense and trade secrets, thus maintains its connection with our everyday life and knowledge. But this simple exercise of reason is largely unavailable to the art public, for art is neither something visible—although its material presence is clearly "seen" —nor something relevant to the everyday experiences of the uninitiated so that one can say something reasonable and intelligent about it. Most people, including myself, have avoided admitting their ignorance and gone along with the expert. Thus, what has been hitherto total nonsense to us in our ordinary frame of mind may emerge as a work of art, with its meaning made perfectly clear to us. Whether the artwork, so expertised, is *really* art is beside the point, for, as we have seen in forgeries, it matters none whether it indeed *is* real art or not.

Whether or not something is a real artwork depends not on the object itself but on the magic wand of the expert.

Little in art depends on the real-ness of the art object itself especially when the matter under consideration has both sides arguing against each other. One side says it is real—or some such argument—and the other says it isn't. Since the definitive existence of art is at the heart of such a situation, it may be advisable for us to examine the situation further.

Beauty pageants are one of those things about which people simply voice their opinions and the one who makes the favorite impression on the judges will win the crown. The judges at beauty pageants are typically chosen from all walks of life—actors, fashion designers, gossip columnists, television personalities, and so on—who are by no means "experts" in beauty. Few people would think choosing the most beautiful requires expertise. Even fewer could come up with any reasonable criteria for defining beauty expertise, much less for defining beauty itself. Consequently no authoritative voice is ever heard on these occasions, nor is a dispute over the best beauty ever settled by calling on experts. Our commonsense tells us that beauty is un-expertisable.

Politics is another such matter. The political arena has no definite criteria—other than the age limit, residency, and a few other such broad qualifications—that limit it to certain qualified persons. In other words, *anyone* can enter politics. We have seen a former tap-dancer, a former actor, a former basketball player, a former football player, a former peanut farmer, and anyone from any number of different backgrounds enter politics and do well. Nor do we necessarily believe that the party out of power is the "wrong" party or the defeated politician an "unreal" politician. No expertise in politics, as in beauty pageants, ever pronounces its oracles in matters political and expects people to heed. People simply express their opinions through ballots and the matter takes its course, totally un-expertised and unaided by expert opinions.

Strangely enough, there is something called "social science" studied in universities which is, in my opinion, also without expertise. No doubt, there are Ph.D.s given, courses taught, researches carried out in the name of social science. But whatever social science may produce as its "knowledge," people pay little or no attention to it unless they want to. If social science in its expert authority says poverty causes crime, people decide on their own whether to accept that wisdom or not. If, on the other hand, people prefer to see it the other way around, say, crime causing poverty, they have every right to override the social science expertise. Either way, it doesn't matter that much. Life goes on unchanged, for life—which is what social science is all about—cannot be made any more livable by expertise. In living, everyone is an expert.

Yes, the reader would have guessed: *Collectible art* is one of those things also, like beauty, politics, and social science, which lacks the definitive quality of reality. Beauty, politics, and social knowledge are all a matter of opinion, and everyone regardless of one's possession or lack of qualification expresses one's opinion freely and aggressively, undeterred by those so-called experts. In all of these areas of life, the ultimate judgment is always left to the popular decision—in a broad sense—of the public at large. In this sense the public is the ultimate judge in such matters that are affairs of taste and policy, and everyone is an "expert," so to speak.

Except, of course, in art.

I have argued that collectible art is really nothing, for in it what is "real" and what is "not real," as seen in forgeries, are intermingled to the extent that it makes no practical difference. In it non-art (forgery) is as much real-art as real-art is non-art.

I have also argued that it is nothing in the sense that we cannot see anything in a typical artwork until the expert tells us what's in the art. In this way collectible art is different from uncollectible art where the public plays the expert, the jury, and the judge.

Collectible art is nothing in another sense as well, when two groups of experts are pitted against each other over the authenticity of Artwork X. The authenticity of Artwork X, of course, has nothing to do with whether it is art or not. Rather, it has to do with whether it is indeed by the artist whose signature appears on the work. But the odd thing about the experts being divided over Artwork X, as seen in Wacker and Van Meegeren, is that once this happens Artwork X *can no longer be real*. How can experts, whose lifetime devotion to the mastery of their profession, be arguing two diametrically opposing points—art vs. non-art—unless either (1) art cannot be defined in terms of "real" or (2) Artwork X is not capable of being decided either way.

The only way out of this dilemma is to assume that the experts—at least some of them—are wrong about their argument. But this assumption cannot be upheld since there is no way to deny their high qualifications, nor can it be decided *which* experts are unqualified. The very fact that they are called upon to decide the case proves their expert qualifications beyond a doubt. But how can two equally-qualified groups of experts argue two *opposite* points about the same object unless the very nature of the object is such that no one can determine what it is? When this happens, the only possible conclusion to draw is that the nature of the object is *immune* to expertise. But, in order to sustain this last point, we must deny the qualifications of experts, which we cannot do. Nor can we deny the expertise of one *group* and grant that of another group, which is impossible to do under the circumstances of recognized expertise. When this dilemma happens on a staggering scale in art, we find it impossible not to question the very assumptions about art's realness.

A psychiatric example comes to mind to amplify this crucial point. Let's say that a group of *highest* qualified psychiatrists have examined Person X's behavior upon the court's request. When the examination is over, a strange thing happens: The best qualified psychiatric experts in the land find themselves divided into two groups with two *diametrically opposed* opinions on Person X. One group says Person X is perfectly healthy; the other group says Person X is perfectly sick. The court will try first to find out if any of the experts—either one group or both—is *un*qualified. But it finds that all of them come with impeccable credentials. Then next the court tries to see if one group can be declared incompetent; this the court finds impossible to do. Thus, the court ends up with two unyielding, diametrically opposed, and highest-qualified opinions on the subject. What is the court to do in this case? What would be the solution for the wisest of judges?

Our reason and commonsense tell us that the court will find it impossible not to throw the case out. As far as the court is concerned, the *case cannot exist* and thus cannot be considered within the known rules of reality. Because it was not expertisable (experts couldn't agree), which was crucial for the disposition of the case, the case *cannot exist!* Hence it has to be thrown out either as nonsense or as "undecidable," in which case the end-result is exactly the same as if the case had been nonexistent. Accordingly, the health-sickness issue, if the above case were true persistently—although it is not—would be utterly irrelevant to our reality. We would have to declare that there is nothing we can do about health and sickness as an issue, for it is a non-issue. Applied to art, the art-no-art issue, hence art itself, would also become irrelevant, for no known human experience, logic or reason can figure it out. It will all have to be declared forever nonexistent or, what amounts to the same conclusion, nothing.

(Obviously, calling Van Goghs or Michelangelos "nothing" requires some explaining, perhaps in a logic that is new to our conventional wisdom. But the "nothingness" of Van Goghs, Michelangelos, Picassos, or Jasper Johns, or whoever else might have painted and have been the subject of controversy, is not as difficult as it first appears. The task, which has somewhat begun so far, requires the entire length of this book and therefore calls for our patience.)

How about a "compromise" between the two groups of psychiatrists so that they could meet somewhere halfway? In this solution, Person X could be declared half-sick and half-healthy. But this solution is an impossible one because the disagreement is mutually exclusive, one being correct making the other necessarily *in*correct. The psychiatric experts were not arguing over "how sick" or "how healthy" Person X's behavior is, but *if* it is sick or healthy. By the same token, all contradictions in art authenticity involve this all-or-nothing proposition. Either Artwork X is "real" in the sense that its signature is identical with its artist, or Artwork X is "not real" in the sense that its signature is done by someone other than the artist. In the practices of art business, these compromises *do* take place in many cases, by making Artwork X "half-done" or "possibly-done" by Van Gogh or Rubens. But that these compromises exist in many instances in art practices does not prove that the contradiction can be resolved that way. It proves, rather, that the art world has decided to live with its logical contradiction and practical corruption, for reasons of simple economics. In this case the dilemma simply shifts from art to art market.

Thus, we can see that the contradiction has been resolved in economics. The art market has resolved to compromise two contradictory elements into a "one-half" solution, in which case Artwork X is now neither art nor non-art, in which case Artwork X cannot possibly be "real" enough to have a definite identity for its existence. How does the market sell non-art as real-art, or, to put it in another way, nothing as something? How does it create reality out of unreality without being accused of being a fraud, sham, or charlatan? What fuels the market in pursuit of the most illusive and most undefinable of all human endeavors?

The problem with the art market is *not* that art is sold as commodities, as some moralists have criticized the practice. But that commodities are sold *as* art. First, though, *some* commodities have to be *created* out of nothingness, and that's where all the explanations of art mystery lie.

Chapter 6

Art is a Possessive Noun

Possession is nine points of the law, the saying goes. So it is in art. To be art is to be possessed, and to love art is to possess it. All collectible artworks begin their career *as art* the moment they become possessed by someone. Conversely, all artworks become instantaneously *possessed* the moment they are recognized as art. No collectible art remains unpossessed. No unpossessed or unpossessable object, however beautiful, on the other hand, is ever thought of as art in a publicly recognized sense. To appreciate art is to possess it or envy those who do possess it. To desire art is to desire its possession. Thus art and its possession act like weights on a balancing pole; the absence of one would make the other fall.

Without this possessability, the idea of art as one's personal property, everything about art as we know it might be very different indeed. Without the possibility of exclusively possessing it in a legal ownership just like any piece of private property, we might have a different notion of art to admire and cherish; the artist might have an entirely different idea of what is to inspire his art; the expert might have a relatively negligible role in the art world; the way the art world assigns value to artworks might have been different or nonexistent; and the kind of behavioral traits and psychology we observe in art-people today may never have materialized. In short, art would never have been the same without possession.

The category of art we defined as "collectible art" would have taken on a totally different meaning and possibly might not even have existed at all, at least not to the extent it does today. It is not unlike a man in a society that has always sold and bought its women as property who can imagine what it would be like to perceive women *without* the notion of possession. Without possession, would he still seek the same virtues in women?; could he "love and respect" them for what they are, without their collectible value?; what *kinds* of women would now be admired and cherished?

Indeed what would art be like in a society that recognizes no value of art as possessable personal property?

33

In the Orient possession of artworks through collection has never been part of its historical past, and its artist has never been the spectacular and heroic individual that he has been in the West. Likewise, without possession and collection, the artist of collectible art in the West—the painter, the sculptor, the native artisan—might have quietly remained nothing more spectacular and heroic than a private poet who expresses himself in unassuming simple verse. In the Orient—and in pre-capitalist Europe—there has never been a dominant artist whose artworks adorn collections, giving honor to their owners, fathering fame and fortune along the way. And the private collectors, those who profess to love, respect, and honor art by possessing them would never exist.

But possessive art is here with us, and so are the collectors. Art existence today is unthinkable without this element of collection and possession, and the modern art world impossible without those who collect and possess artworks.

Laurie Adams tells of a trial in the 20s that brought the issue of "What is art?" to the forefront when a sculpture's "art-ness" was questioned by the customs officials over its entry taxes, which would be smaller if the object was regarded as a work of art. Various art experts gave the following testimony to that issue: To summarize it briefly,

Edward Steichen: Form and balance, something that is achieved in the mind of the (artist), harmonious lines, has proportion, etc.

Jacob Epstein: Pleases my sense of beauty: a feeling of pleasure; a beautiful object, etc.

Forbes Watson: The form, the balance, the beautiful sense of workmanship, etc.

Frank Crowninshield: Its proportions, its form, its balance, the design, the workmanship, etc.

William Henry Fox: Has expression, form, registering an idea, etc.

Henry McBride: Excites in me a sense of beauty and appeals to my imagination, etc.

All of these gentlemen, art experts of the highest order of the time, might have done their best to answer the question. But their descriptions of art— "beauty," "form," "imagination" and so on—although perfectly harmless "pseudo-intellectual waffle" as an art critic has observed, are so abstract that to define art through these descriptions is like looking for a missing person by giving the descriptions of four limbs, two eyes, one nose, one mouth, with hair on the head. Idle philosophers may raise the question of "What is art?" and be satisfied with such idle answers as are given above. But the question is almost *never* raised as an idle question, for it is almost always raised in a specific context for a specific answer: Namely, is this object in front of us a work of art or not? Whether it is (or is not) because it has (or has not) "beauty," "form," or "imagination" does not help this pressing question that seeks a practical, definite answer.

The best answer, avoiding all this mumbo-jumbo, is arrived at by simply asking this: Is the object *wanted* as a work of art by someone who is willing to *pay* the price, however large or small? If the answer is yes, then it is a work of art; if the answer is no, then it is *not* a work of art. What is art? The answer now is simple: Any object that is *wanted by someone as art*. I don't mean to be cynical about the whole business of art in looking at it this way, but I find no other reasonable way to define it. Let me explain.

Traditionally we tend to think people want Object X because Object X is desirable in some way—beautiful, valuable, lovely, whatever. But that is not necessarily so. What we often fail to recognize, especially in the case of collectible art, is that it can work *the other way around*. That is, Object X *becomes* "beautiful," "precious," or "lovely" precisely because it is *wanted*. Why something is wanted in the first place runs a whole gamut of human psychology, little or none of which has anything to do with art, though much with art collection. In its elementary form, human psychology is a strange thing. *Anything* can become an object as "beautiful," "precious," "lovely," or whatever. Since no one knows for sure what art is, the experts' nonsense cited above notwithstanding, anything wanted, desired, and collected *as art* must be thought of as art. Can *anything* become a desired object of art? As we have seen, the answer is yes: Anything can become the object of "beautiful," "precious," or "lovely" adulation. Just recall the Andy Warhol "Art Collections" bonanza of 1988 which netted 25 million dollars.

Conversely, and this is an important question to consider, are all things that are beautiful, precious, or lovely avidly *wanted* by people? Not necessarily. Then which objects that are beautiful, precious, or lovely are desired and which are *not*? A sunset is beautiful but no one gets terribly excited about its photographs or paintings. Air is precious but no one wants to "collect" it in a bottle and brag about it to others. Flowers are lovely but our desire for them is fairly lukewarm and occasional. Why then, if they are beautiful, precious, or lovely, aren't they eagerly wanted? But that's getting a little ahead of ourselves. Let's get back to the direct subject of possession *as art*.

Artwork X maintains its "art-ness" not by having beauty, form, or imagination but by rendering itself "desired" or "wanted." To a collector, the desirability and wantedness of Artwork X is always proportional to the expensiveness of Artwork X. Its expensiveness is then maintained by its exclusiveness, allowing no competition in the market—hence that hostility toward forgeries or "unauthorized" copies. Thus, once the process is set in motion, the art-ness of Artwork X is practically self-perpetuating and indestructible. It is wanted and desired because it is expensive; it is expensive because it is exclusive—no one else can have it; and because it is exclusive it is wanted and desired for possession.

This cycle has nothing to do with art and everything to do with human psychology. Why is Artwork X so desired and wanted in the first place? The answer is two-fold: It is very expensive; and it is in somebody else's possession. Or, conversely, Artwork X is in *someone* else's possession but it *could* become one's own possession. Or, to put it in another way, it is in *one's own* possession which someone *else* wants for his collection. This simple fact makes every artwork an object of desirability, keeps every art collector one heartbeat away from a great triumph, and renders art selling and buying dynamic, exciting, and addictive.

It is for this reason of simple human psychology that art collectors want everyone to *know* that they own such and such artworks, just to heighten the desirability. Possessing something beautiful, precious, or lovely and *no one* knowing about it would be the most unbearable torture for any art collector. To put it in another way, Artwork X's art-ness, hence its desirability, would instantly fall to zero the moment it is known that, for some reason, it cannot be possessed—like the Washington Monument or the Grand Canyon—or is so common that it is not worth possessing—such as an unlimited number of "Van Goghs" priced at five to ten dollars a piece. In this case, no amount of beauty, preciousness, or loveliness in the object would be able to entice the collector's desire to possess it.

Listen to the chairman of Sotheby's who said, as quoted in Robert Wraight's book mentioned earlier: "Without covetousness [translation: possession] you are not going to have an appreciation of art. And I think that if covetousness by some magic was destroyed art would come to an end. It's very rare to be able to appreciate art without wanting to own it." Or, quoting Gerald Reitlinger, "To collect nothing at all is to descend below the level of magpies and marmots." Thus unmasked, Konstantin Bazarov is more blunt about the art collector's love for art: "A lot of so-called art appreciation is totally bogus."

Where art appreciation means art possession, the rest of us must now be content with watching sunsets, clouds, or flowers, and buying cheap landscape pictures from local illustrators for our walls. But no one with his right mind would call us "art lovers" although we enjoy beautiful things, or "art collectors" although we do indeed buy and use these adornments. For art loving and art collecting cannot be conceived of without the exclusive possession of expensive artworks which the terms imply. Loving beautiful things does not qualify one as an art lover; possessing them does. Buying artworks does not qualify one as an art collector; buying expensive ones does. And with one additional important difference: That the collector *cannot* enjoy the beauty of his collected art because he is overwhelmed by the pleasure of possession, whereas the rest of us can and do enjoy every bit of art we love and buy.

(Incidentally, I am deliberately leaving out the consideration of certain "utilitarian" functions of art objects, such as using art in interior decorations, covering walls with pretty but inconsequential pictures, public places filling their space with inconspicuous objects, and so on. They are all intended as one-time users of art objects and are not subject to the dynamics of art collection. Hence, they stand outside the current discussion of collectible art.)

Corollary to the above factor of possession is its flip-side effect, a factor only reluctantly acknowledged among collectors but nevertheless significant as a motivating force in their activity: That is *the pleasure of denying* the others from enjoying what one possesses. The more expensive an artwork, consequently, the greater the particular reason for art possession. It is difficult to tell which factor gives the collector greater pleasure, his own possession or the other's dispossession. But in every art object collected and possessed this double-pleasure factor exists, giving the collector every reason to look forward to the next round of possession-dispossession contest. Only the less-financially-secure or the unabashed philistine would buy and sell artworks for financial gains and as tax write-offs. Among the latter, though quite numerous in the collection business, their pleasure is only one-sided, that is, the pleasure of one's own possession—either in profit or in tax deduction—, but not the important point of giving the other collector the pain of envy and dispossession. Few genuine art collectors would consider collecting an artwork that does not produce this negative effect. Those art-people who collect artworks do not search for things beautiful or artistic. They search for things to possess that others would also want to possess.

Aside from the few idle and thoroughly inconsequential philosophers who speculate on this or that aspect of art with no appreciable effect on the real art world, everyone else in academic art is partaking in some aspect of art selling and buying for the express purpose of someone's possession. "Art theory," "art history" and any number of such lofty-sounding scholarly expositions, while seemingly academic and unrelated to the knitty-gritty of art collection, have to do with the rise of one collectible art school and decline of another, the increased desirability for one artist's works and the decreased desirability for another, and so on. When an art professor lectures on art, he is lecturing on art collection; when an art critic expounds on this "ism" and that, he is talking about the trends in the collectability of certain artworks; when an art authority examines an artwork for a collector or a dealer and gives his pronouncement, he is determining the art-price, thereby the degree of pleasure associated with its possession; when an art-book publisher prints a handsomely bound art history book, he is simply compiling the most highly-priced and sought-after artworks in the market. Thus, there is no such thing as art scholarship that is not really the scholarship of art collection. In this sense, all art scholars function as the servants of art collectors. Their activity is deeply intertwined with the art market and their service is an integral part of the selling and buying of art.

Likewise in collectible art there is no such thing as purely "academic" art disputes. There has never been an "art controversy" that is not related to price, reputation, or status in art—the common elements that affect the desirability and possessability of an artwork. The controversy of art definitions quoted above was triggered by the owner's refusal to pay import taxes on the grounds that it was an artwork and the U.S. customs office's insistence that it was not. Other celebrated cases in art history in which experts have given their opinions on whether anything is "real art" or not or how real—such as the Mark Rothko case, two portraits by Leonardo disputed by both owners as to their genuineness, or the Whistler vs. Ruskin case in which the latter destroyed the former's art value by criticizing it, and so on—are the controversies of collection. Not one single purely *aesthetic* controversy was, nor can be, ever resolved in a court of law.

The reader might note that such controversies of art money almost never arise in uncollectible forms of art. Disputes as to "how good" a particular art school or artwork is may arise on occasion, but the disputants generally tend to leave the issue to the good judgment of history and posterity. It would have been unthinkable during the late nineteenth century for the two contending schools of music—the Wagnerian and the Brahmsian schools—to try to resolve their differences in court, calling in music experts to prove their point. It is unthinkable because there was no dispute involving the utterly serious possession or money related to each art school or artwork that is in dispute and could be resolved in that fashion.

It is totally unsurprising then to know that there is no such thing as "aesthetic" pleasure in collectible art. As purely aesthetic pleasure, one could be thinking of a beautiful sunset, a cloud, or a flower, as a child would delight in things sweet and comforting. Those who enjoy such things only because they are pleasurable to look at may claim genuine love for aesthetic pleasures in things beautiful. But they are not part of art-people in the art establishment so far examined and certainly not part of our present consideration. The gulf between those who *love* beautiful things and those who *collect* beautiful things is so great, and it renders them so alien to each other, that they have not one shred of common ground between them as lovers of beautiful things.

Nor, more significantly perhaps, is there any conceivable similarity between those who love collectiable art and those the love *un*collectible art. The latter are those who love art in music, literature, drama, philosophy, or whatever, simply because they enjoy the pleasure of these particular artforms and their representative repertoire. What little money they spend on tickets to performances, on book purchases, or buying recordings, and so forth, is almost wholly negligible. The pleasure from uncollectible art is all purely and simply "artistic" since there is no other consideration in this pleasure. No lover of uncollectible art will brag about a new Georgi Solti recording of the "Ninth" he just bought; he will just enjoy it by *listening* to it. And unless he liked the music for itself he wouldn't have purchased it in the first place.

Those who love collectible art, as we have seen, on the other hand, have only one thing utmost on their minds: To possess it so that no one else can have it. The pleasure of the artwork itself is almost wholly negligible. I say the word negligible with some confidence. Can we imagine taking the high-brow art collector to a sunset, to a cloud, or to a flower and see him thoroughly *enjoy* the beauty in these things? If we argue about the "beauty" of the sunset, the cloud, or the flower, the collector would be impressively uncomprehending about the "beauty" part. He might admit frankly that he is *not* in the beauty business: HE IS IN THE COLLECTION BUSINESS! They have nothing to do with each other. There may be exceptions to this caricatured image of the typical collector. But the exceptions are so rare that they become meaningless in the larger scheme of art and merit only a passing remark.

So let me highlight the difference between the two kinds of art and two varieties of "art lovers" thusly: Those who profess to love collectible art then proceed to *enslave* what they profess to love; those who profess to love uncollectible art then proceed to *liberate* what they profess to love.

Let's look at this point with some care, for the former's desire to enslave art reveals another strange and bizarre element in the behavior of art-people and their art world that's different from our own ordinary world and its logic.

Chapter 7

Art, Women, and Butterflies

It is common human instinct to share with others that which we truly enjoy. When we see a beautiful sunset, we immediately think of *someone else* with whom we wish to share it in our collective admiration. When we find a great book, similarly, we want *other people* to read it too. When we hear an excellent symphony, we recommend it to our friends and sometimes even strangers. The more people that can enjoy what we find enjoyable, the greater our *own* enjoyment. That is human nature regarding all things we truly love and respect: We want it spread around to make as many people happy as possible.

Except, of course, in collectible art.

The instinct of an art collector is precisely the *opposite* of all normal human response: The collector wants to own an artwork so that no one else can have its enjoyment and looks for ways to possess it exclusively for himself. Like a pathologically spoiled child who owns many toys, he doesn't want anybody else to have the pleasure of playing with them. This is what I meant when I said art collectors enslave art through private ownership.

The strange psychology of art collection can be understood more clearly when we understand the true nature of "collection." Art and collection have become so intertwined, actually one and the same, that British psychologist Nicholas Humphrey explained the origin of art in *terms* of the human instinct to "collect." The nature of collection then can best be understood when we consider the nature of what is *being collected*. What are indeed the things that we deem worth collecting?

Broadly speaking, there are three categories of collection: First, as a hobby (stamps, bottle caps, antiques, gems, etc.); second, for investment (stocks, bonds, treasury bills, jewelries, etc); and third, for status (collectible artworks in painting, sculpture, native art, rare objects, beautiful-but-subservient women, precious jewelries, etc.) Notice that, of the three categories, there is no place for "art collection."

While we have been saying that art and collection are synonymous, what makes this practice so strange and bizarre is that IF OBJECT X

IS ART, IT CANNOT BE COLLECTED!. Conversely, what is collected *cannot* be art. How is it so?

The answer is as follows: If we understand, as collectors claim, that art evokes a wonderful feeling in us, then what we instinctively desire to do is to *spread* that feeling by *sharing* it. We do not want to enslave what we truly love and respect, unless, as noted, we are pathologically spoiled and full of possessiveness.

Notice also above that the first and second categories for collecting things—hobbies and investments—are all *practical, utilitarian,* and therefore *rational* ones, perfectly justifiable within themselves without having to invoke the rhetoric of "beauty" or "love." One collects stamps or stocks either for pure enjoyment or for profit. Further justification is unnecessary. But why do people collect art?

Collecting art has to do with neither hobby nor profit. For it to be a hobby, the collector must know something about art. As a for-profit venture, it is too risky and low-yielding. But what are the things that are collected for the reason of status? We observe art, women, jewelry, and so on. But how does the collector "feel" toward his collections? We would say, pride. What is he proud *of?* What he is proud of is the *fact* that he has them in *his* collection. Since we do not want to exclusively possess what we truly love and respect, art cannot possibly be collected for the reasons of love and respect. Then, for *what* reason? What really is it that is collected, giving the owner a sense of pride and status? Why, none other than pure and simple contempt!

In other words, the essential psychology of art collection is based on nothing but contempt for art. Neither love nor respect could induce anyone to collect what is loved and respected by him. Only the things we *use* to gain social status and possessive satisfaction are we ever inclined to possess wholly. Only the things we have contempt for, not things we love and respect, are we ever inclined to keep under lock and key. Contrary to what the art world has been saying, ART AND COLLECTION are in fact mutually *exclusive:* If it is art, it is not collected. If it is collected, it is not art.

Art collected is like a pretty woman, just pretty with no other redeeming value, that men will display for status and pride with no intrinsic utilitarian function in her. They may adorn her with great jewelry and pomp, but is she really loved and respected by men? Only those men who have a contemptuous attitude toward women would think of using her that way. If the men truly loved and respected her, they would never think of enslaving her by private possession. In spite of what these men may profess about their pretty women, they do not know how to love. In fact, they are women-haters. Those who truly love art would simply admire it and then want to share the experience with other art lovers. True art lovers *cannot* be art collectors. Art collectors are art-haters in truth and slave-owners in their attitudes toward their collected art. If an artwork could speak, this is what it would tell its collector-possessor-owner: If you truly love me and respect me, as you say you do, please set me free!

In what is called art appreciation, like the pathological, women-hating butterfly collector who also "collects" women and tortures them in his private dungeon in John Fowler's novel aptly titled *The Collector*, we see really nothing but enslavement, contempt, and hatred. It is a strange and bizarre twist for art loving and art collecting, which were always thought to be one and the same. People who simply criticize the art establishment for its greed miss the mark entirely. It is not greed that moves and shakes the art world, although small-timers do pursue profits through art investments. It is the undercurrent of possessive pathology in contempt and hatred which drives men and women to their collecting binge. Accordingly, we should admire people who buy and sell artworks for strictly economic reasons. Although they are no doubt philistines of money-grabbing and vulgar pursuers of profit in any way they can, these economic traders of art have a healthy *respect* (if not love) for the commodities they trade. At least they make no bones about the purpose of their art business, for it is *business*, and nothing else. As such, they treat art as a valuable commodity with the respect that it deserves. These economic art collectors do not pretend to be art connoisseurs, nor do they profess to love, respect, and honor art beyond their business interests.

If we are still inclined to associate art collection with love for art, we should ask this simple question: How can one have true love and respect for what is in one's *collection*? Could one truly love and respect Jesus Christ if he were in one's exclusive possession under one's private contract and legal ownership, in which no one but himself had the right to enjoy? If one truly loved and respected Jesus Christ, would one *want* to collect and possess him exclusively and privately so that no one else can share the benefit?

In many ways, the typical art collector displays many of the character traits of a pathological hater or a spoiled brat who tortures whatever—or often whomever—is unfortunate enough to fall into his possession. He plays with it, torments it at his whims, or locks it up at will. At no time would he display any *genuine* love or respect or affection for it while it is under his control and in his possession. Art or no art, to be possessed by someone is to be treated with utmost contempt. It is the very psychology of possession, from which such cruel behavioral traits and thought patterns are possible. No collector or bratty child would want to own a slave only to love and respect and honor him or set him free.

What is true in all collectible art, as we have seen, is that nothing is considered worthwhile art unless it is possessed by someone. Conversely, no worthwhile art remains unpossessed by someone. But, as we now know, the moment art becomes possessed in someone's exclusive collection it *ceases* to be art and instantly becomes an object of contempt and enslavement. Some people might say this is the fate of all things bought and sold, but those who buy and sell art for investment do not treat art with the collector's possessive contempt.

Here is then the essence of the dilemma that art faces in our society: To be art, it must be possessed by someone with a specific price associated with it. But to be possessed and be in someone's private collection is to cease to be art. We have no other "public" definition of art since it has always been associated with collection, price, and possession. It is like a pretty woman saying to a man: If you truly love me, respect me, and honor me, then buy me, collect me, and possess me. It would be an utter illusion to believe that buying, collecting, and possessing could maintain the love, respect, and honor for that which is bought, collected, and possessed.

Since all art in someone's possession has no specific reference other than price—all else can be argued, but the price remains specific—, the fact that it is in someone's collection overrides all other facts about it. It is always that a specific artwork is part of a specific collection; or that such and such a collector *owns* such and such artworks, one giving the other a status recognition depending on who is more famous, the art or the collector. If the artwork is more famous it gives a status lift to its collector; if the collection is more prestigious it makes its collected artwork famous by being part of it. A Michelangelo makes Rockefeller's collection more prestigious; a Guggenheim collection makes a lesser artist or artwork instantly credible.

But this fact of collection, which establishes art's worth, value, reputation, is the very thing that also *trivializes* it as art, indistinguishable from all the other objects that people collect. Nowadays *anything* can be the subject of collection. The fact that art is also collected or, conversely, what is collected happens to be art, is just coincidental. Suppose the collector who purchased the well-publicized Van Gogh ("Irises") for close to 50 million dollars also purchased a rare red sapphire for the same amount of money. Would the collector show any particularly different kind of love, respect, and honor for the Van Gogh than that shown toward the red sapphire? To the one who *bought, collected,* and *possessed* the Van Gogh, why would the Van Gogh be any different from the red sapphire or, for that matter, *anything* else that costs the same amount of money and hence has the same value?

Thus, artworks that fall into private collections must contend with all sorts of collectible objects that are anti-art, pseudo-art, and non-art, with no particularly privileged position accorded to it *as* art. The very process of collection—price, money, ownership—nullifies this distinction, like the noblewoman of distinction who has fallen on hard times and must now compete as a means for survival to get into someone's employment. Once the price is decided, all collected items—or employed persons—are considered only according to the price paid for the collection and privatization. It would be laughable if the noblewoman, hired to work in the kitchen, would act superior to other kitchen employees with the same pay just because she was from a noble family. She might have been superior with her nobility *before* her current employment, but no longer. The price of her employment has nullified all the distinctions of her nobility which she might have possessed before.

But the very act of art possession imposes another strain on art. In order for art to exist, it must be possessed; but in order to be possessed, art must stand out and be noticed among the many contending artworks and non-artworks. The precondition of possessability makes it impossible to treat all artworks equally. There are too many pieces of art and not enough art collectors. It becomes essential or, rather, imperative in the art world that some artworks must necessarily become *over-priced* and other artworks *under-priced* to maintain the system of collection. If art were simply art in some publicly defined way and left at that without the factors of money and possession, no artwork would be over-priced or under-priced vis a vis other artworks. The only question left would be which of the artworks can stand the test of time, through history and posterity. Of course, this question has nothing to do with pricing. But, since art collection is unthinkable to us without a specific price-tag, it becomes absolutely necessary that some artworks are selected as special and therefore specially-priced, while other artworks are ignored and thought of as unworthy of collection.

In other words, some artworks must be *made* special, above all the others, in order to keep the business of art collection going. Hence, the obsessive and often comical attachment to the *name* of the artist in the art world.

It now transpires that what the collectors are seeking is not really art. What they want is the recognizable name, not how good the work is. It is the signature that matters and this fact is responsible for the cosmically catastrophic proportion of forgeries among the real artworks. Once the name is forged, the artwork can pass for real quite easily.

Chapter 8

Name is the Name of the Game

Virtually every "art controversy" arises over the question of identity: "Is Artwork X really art?" But the *real* issue to be settled is: "Is Artwork X really by Artist Y?" To us, these would seem two separate questions, one involving the artistic question and the other the technical question of mere identity. In the strange world of art, however, the artistic question is settled by the technical answer. In other words, *who* painted Artwork X determines *how good* or *how real* Artwork X is.

Because the question to be settled is a technical one—that of identifying the painter—not the painting, the answer it seeks is also a technical one—that of *whether or not* Artwork X is real, assuming that it is an either-or proposition. Either it is real by being verified of its painter's identity, or it is considered unreal when this verification test proves unsatisfactory.

Oddly enough, however, the fact that Artwork X in dispute may be "close enough" so that it *could* have been done by Artist Y matters little or nothing in the strange world of art selling and art buying. This all-or-nothing struggle is waged not only between forgeries and "real" art, but also among "real" artworks.

Writer Ann Waldron asks, "Why is a picture worth millions when the experts think Rembrandt painted it and not worth ten dollars when it turns out it was forged?" The answer she provides is interesting: "It is, of course, a lie to say that a picture painted by an art student is a Rembrandt, just as it is a lie to say that a ring is gold if it is made of brass." But there are several problems in Waldron's observation: When is a Rembrandt a Rembrandt? If "the experts think Rembrandt painted it" isn't it a Rembrandt? Not just when it "turns out it was forged," as she puts it, but *how* does it "turn out?" Did the picture just fall apart, turn suddenly ugly, change composition *after* the experts had verified it as a genuine Rembrandt? She says brass is not gold and a forgery not real art. But can they be compared? Gold and brass can easily be told apart, but can the same be said for real art and forgeries?

(On the other hand, there is such a thing as the truth in its own right that should be pursued. "There is among scholars, of course, a disinterested desire to get at the truth in such cases," observes another writer Robert Wraight for a possible explanation. But truth deserves to be pursued only if the *consequences* of the truth are important. Obviously, there is no such importance in art and forgery.)

Why is art an all-or-nothing proposition? When the "Christ's Head" was discovered to have been done by Van Meegeren the forger, and not by Vermeer as previously believed—after the forger's confession—, the painting dropped in market value from $220,000 to $5 after the discovery that Vermeer's signature was actually Van Meegeren's. Why didn't the price—and presumably the artwork's artistic value—go down just a little, say by a thousand dollars or two, since the forged signature is the only thing wrong with it and is the least significant part of the whole painting? What fantastic illogic!

Similarly, the forgers who had become famous with their exploits— de Hory, Dossena, Keating, for example—suffered drastically when they produced the very same quality artworks under their *own* names. Collectors wouldn't pay anything for them. Even the whisper of inauthenticity here, or a doubtful statement there, sends the price plunging. When the authenticity of some Rembrandts—all of them among big-time collections—was questioned recently, their market value dropped radically. Few collectors and experts are interested in the question of "how good" Artwork X is. Their artistic interest remains largely on the question of whose "name" appears on the canvas.

Collectors are willing to pay high sums for a big name—sometimes ridiculously high sums—, regardless of how good the artwork is. But these collectors would offer practically nothing if the name is "wrong." But, why is even the worst of a big name considered so much better than the best of a no name?

Since art cannot be possible without collection, at least in the way it is understood today, art must be collected to be art. But there is much *too much* art being produced (why so much art is produced is another question to be dealt with later), and not all of it can be collected and possessed in a marketplace through its usual competitive mechanism. The art market is not an ordinary market. It is a closed market, closed to only a few artworks that it considers to be commodities. The almost-unlimited production capacity cannot be matched by the severely-limited collection capacity. The art world would rather deal with one 50 million dollar Van Gogh than with five million works by no-names at 10 dollars a piece.

Art is neither mass-produced by machines, nor mass-consumed by the public. Since art consumption is never vital to human survival or daily comfort, it cannot be pushed or advertised to clear the deck. Hence the problem of over-production (too many artists) and under-consumption (too few collectors) in the art world. The art world's solution to this problem has always been: SELECTION OF A FEW SPECIAL NAMES OVER MANY NO NAMES.

What is art history? many have asked. Art history is really the history of big-name selection for collection and possession purposes, nothing more, nothing less. Why? Unlike the artists of uncollectable art who leave only their art as their legacy, the big names of collectable art leave big collections. No two legacies within the same field can be more contradictory to each other than collectable art and uncollectable art. It is one of those supreme human errors that have come to call both endeavors art. For collectable artists do not produce artworks; they produce collections.

The selection of few over many, then, is crucial to the continuing existence and prosperity of the art world, if not art itself. While uncollectible art is quietly being enjoyed in someone's reading room, or at a public concert hall, or on a stage, or simply as a reflection of the mind, collectible art is resented as a massive, media-hyped spectacle of *collecting* and *possessing*. It is not the pleasure of looking at the "Mona Lisa" or the "Irises," but the spectacle of how much money is involved with such artworks—in price, in insurance premium, etc.—that is primarily associated with such artworks. In other words, "art appreciation" notwithstanding, the pleasure of such collectible art amounts to little more than the pleasure of GOSSIPING ABOUT IT. Therefore, the status of collectible art is always that of celebrity, almost always linked to money and gossiping.

The problem in this big-name philosophy is twofold: First, what is collected in someone's private possession is absolutely useless to the rest of the world. Even a museum collection doesn't help, where such is available, for very few people can manage to go to a museum often enough. Since the main, if not the sole, purpose of private collection is to keep artworks from being seen by others, with public museums gradually being priced out of competition, there is not much surprising about this consequence of art collection. What to do about this problem intrinsic to collectible art is yet to be discussed, but in the meantime let's deal with the second problem which is our concern now.

It is the way the art market promotes a few big pictures as "great" art at the expense of many that remain wholly neglected. In this way art business—not art itself—may continue and prosper. But this imperative in art business requires a considerable leap in logic and commonsense. For, as noted above, this philosophy of all-or-nothing assumes that some artworks are everything whereas many are no art at all. How could that be? Unlike the art controversies over name-identification, no artwork is ever everything or nothing, or real art or non-art. As in everything else that embodies different degrees of quality, different artworks may be ranked according to their artistic merits, one artwork being considered "better" or "worse" than another, and so on. But never should an artwork be considered "non-art," especially in view of the fact that fairly straightforward "nothings" have been known—like the empty canvas by Jo Baer—to be classified as "great art." With this in mind, it is indeed puzzling for us to think that the art world would select few as everything (millions of dollars) and many as nothing (not even a dollar). There is no other way of judging what art is, at least in the collectible art world, leaving the amount of money collectors are willing to pay as the only qualifying criterion. If an insignificant sketch by a Leonardo is collected for one million dollars, why wouldn't a work close to it in quality be something slightly *less* than that amount, say, 900,000 dollars, or perhaps 800,000 dollars? If Van Gogh's "Irises" are worth 50 million dollars, why couldn't somebody paint a work close to it in quality for a price slightly less than that, the difference in price being proportional to the difference in quality?

It is worth speculating what kinds of artworks those big time museums would display if the "name-factor" were entirely removed from consideration. We may assume that their exhibitions—now free from famous names as criteria—may be very different as a result. (We may recall the Van Meegeren incident when a committee of experts recommended purchase of a forgery only because it bore the famous name, although none "liked it very much.")

The seeming illogic can be resolved, however, if we see it as intrinsic to the myths of art, that art is something we cannot logically and sensibly discuss. Many people would agree with such a view of art. The problem with this view is that such mythical notions of art and the artist do *not* apply in the more rational and cold-eyed world of money, price, and collection. Art itself may be as mysterious as it is cracked up to be in the popular imagination and historical biographies, but I don't believe the *art market* is. The art market, not unlike other markets, has one purpose for its existence: To sell and buy its commodities. Even the misty-eyed art lover in the end must pull out his checkbook and pay for his misty-eyed art mystery. Besides, unlike in uncollectible art, one does not just admire a collectible artwork; one admires an artwork by *collecting* it; one collects it by *paying* for it.

The main mechanism by which the art world satisfies the requirement of collection, as mentioned, is the selection of few names as everything and the neglect of many as nothing. Robert Wraight has observed that "Today, more than ever before, it's the name that counts." "What's in a name?" asks Van Meegeren's biographer John Godley. His own answer:

"Almost everything." Fernand Legos, de Hory's voracious accomplice, expresses a similar sentiment when he says, "Only the famous is worth selling." Why such an obsession with the name of the artist, not the artistic substance?

There are two reasons for the crucial name factor in collectible art, which explain much of the myth in collectible art and art business. The first, an *economic* one, is that the market cannot sell everything that is produced and the collector cannot collect everything that is produced. The second, which we might call *substantive* factor, perhaps more important than the first, is intrinsic to the very nature of collectible art, namely, its "nothing-ness" in substance. In short, only where substance is lacking or unclear is the name considered crucial. Let's look at these two factors more critically.

To look at the economic factor first. There are two common ways in which the price of artworks can be affected. One is the question of authenticity, as we have seen above, and the other is the *volume* of the works available on the market.

From the art market's point of view, it makes perfect sense that people want to buy and possess the real thing. But what *is* the real thing in collectible art? The price plummets from millions to ten dollars, as Waldron observed above, because the *signature*, not the picture itself, is wrong. It makes absolutely no sense to one who is neither so passionately devoted to art collection nor devoured by the possessive urges. It is the same Rembrandt that stares at you whether it is by Rembrandt himself or by an impostor, the picture never changes anything. If it was a beautiful picture as a Rembrandt, worth millions of dollars, it is still a beautiful picture as a non-Rembrandt, but now worth ten dollars. Only those who make little use of reason and innocent children would take such an insignificant factor so seriously and not notice the contradiction.

The volume of artworks on the market can affect the price adversely. Because it is absolutely necessary for the art market to deal with as *few* artworks as possible, the price of each art commodity tends to be exorbitant, often extraordinary. More often than not, an artwork becomes important as art by simply costing an extraordinary price. When asked why he sold his forgeries at such high prices, Van Meegeren testified in court: "I had to. If I had sold them at a low price, they would have been at once recognized as fakes." The psychological factor of the pleasure of denying others from enjoying the work, not the pleasure of enjoying the artwork itself, being an essential motive for art possession, it is crucial that the art market must keep as few expensive artworks in circulation as possible.

This is also true even for a well known artist. As too many artworks in circulation as a whole are bad for the art business, too many artworks produced by one artist are equally bad for their price. Christopher Wright observes that La Tour suffered a "black period" in the 50s and 60s when paintings attributed to him "grew alarmingly" to "a truly spectacular increase to about forty pictures." Only in the comic and insane world of collectible art, incidentally, would we equate new discoveries of master artworks with disasters. One of the greatest fears of all art collectors, indeed, is the specter of the world discovering more artworks by the artists who are in their collections, making them less exclusive. Only in collectible art would these additional artistic triumphs spell disasters for the artist. The collectors want their own collections to be the only ones in existence, desperately hoping that the rest of the world, especially their fellow competing collectors, would never get to enjoy what they possess. Deep down, they would rejoice to no end if all the artworks in the rest of the world, except theirs, would somehow disappear or be destroyed, leaving them as the only collector in the world to possess artworks. It is for this reason alone that I believe art collectors are really art-haters at heart.

On the other hand, this is not so in uncollectible art. If we suddenly discovered five more plays by Shakespeare, two more symphonies by Beethoven, one more novel by Stendhal, or four more dialogues by Plato, all authenticated by their quality, not names, their reputation would only increase and no one would say their output "grew alarmingly." The world would rejoice at the discovery, the artists' reputation would soar higher, and art lovers all over would enjoy the newly discovered masterworks.

But why the gloom and doom in collectible art with the increased number of masterpieces? The answer is easy enough to get: Because collectible art is a "collectible" first and art next. The fewer in existence, the market principle goes, the better is the price. It has nothing to do with art and everything to do with the market and collection. When Mark Rothko's paintings were contested between his trustees and his family after his death, Laurie Adams writes, a party to the case feared "Rothko's market might suffer as a result of litigation and the resultant public knowledge that 798 of his pictures were available."

It is a small wonder that the art market is desperate to keep its circulation as small as possible, which is quite contrary to the regular marketplace where the larger the volume of sale, the better it is for everyone. If art is a good thing, it would seem, more of a good thing is not necessarily better in collectible art. This is another reason why I think art collection is basically an act that produces anti-art consequences.

The second factor, the *substantive* reason for the obsessive importance attached to name in art, is more serious because it has to do with art's reason for being. In collectible art, because substance is lacking or absent, name has to take the place of substance. In other words, name goes *in place* of substance.

The absurdity of name over substance is not so difficult to observe around us in everyday life. Many people go for "name brands" in consumer goods. But who are they? Only the most empty-headed among us—superficial television watchers, impressionable teenagers, shallow name-droppers, gullible "bird-brains," the idle rich with money to burn—would go after the name when there is no substantive reason for the choice. The principle of name over substance is simply that what is on the surface passes for what is real. If it is a "Van Gogh," go for it; if it is a "Rembrandt," buy it. The collector who professes to love art, if asked about his collections, would give a string of "big names" that belong to his collections. Never mind that some of them are probably forgeries. The sequel to Margaret Mitchell's "Gone With the Wind" was sold for 5 million dollars, to be written by a contemporary author, *even before one word has been written*! Why? Because of the name: Margaret Mitchell, "Gone With the Wind," Scarlet O'Hara, Rhett Butler, Ashley Wilkes, Melanie Hamilton...

Name is *everything* only where substance is *nothing*. *Who* painted that particular picture is important if the picture itself is *un*important. It is somewhat analogous to the importance of the anchorman on television news when the news itself isn't important. Even after years of popular display, suddenly an artwork is withdrawn from public exhibition once the name has been decided wrong, as in the case of Van Meegeren's Vermeer at the Boymans, as if the *artwork* itself matters nothing, only the name of the artist. The Van Meegeren-Vermeer had been the highlight of the Queen's Fortieth Jubilee and "the spiritual focus of the exhibition, despite the distinguished works by Rembrandt, Hals, and Grunwald" at the same exhibition. Exasperated at this incongruity, Van Meegeren's sympathetic biographer John Godley observed that "Perhaps the only standard by which the value of a picture should be judged is its artistic merit."

But the truth is that the "artistic merit" that Godley speaks of does not exist in collectible art. The obsession with name is both the effect and proof of the nonexistent and impossible "artistic merit." There is no way to judge artistic merit in collectible art, viewed simply from the number of forgeries that exist among supposedly real artworks. If there *were* artistic merit intrinsic to *each artwork* that can stand on its own, why would we need name-attribution as central to art value? If there *were* independent artistic merit in each artwork that can be independently judged, why would we have so many forgeries among them? If the most awe-inspiring frescoes by Michelangelo and the most-nothing in Jo Baer's "empty canvas" are both considered art, how *could* there be any artistic merit in any artwork?

In uncollectible art, by contrast and to give ourselves some perspective in the matter, no famous artist, neither a Shakespeare nor a Beethoven, relies on his name to carry the weight. There are plays by Shakespeare and compositions by Beethoven, because of the lack of their artistic merit or whatever, that languish in the shadow of other more meritorious works despite the fact that they bear the famous name as their authors. In fact, many of the works by famous artists now stand largely forgotten because of their inferior quality as seen by history and public judgment. When a new symphony by Mozart, composed when he was relatively young, was discovered the reaction to it was more one of curiosity than ecstasy. Its subsequent reception proved that the name of its famous composer had no effect on its artistic merit; it was just an early student piece surpassed by the composer's later works. (That's why forgeries in music or literature are rare, almost nonexistent.) In uncollectible art, it is art that makes the artist famous. In collectible art, it is the name that makes the artwork famous.

If the above discovery were a new painting—even a student piece— by Michelangelo, on the other hand, the most ardent collectors of the world, even before seeing it—as in the "Gone With the Wind" episode— , would have bid for it solely on the basis that its artist was *Michelangelo*. Such absurdity is possible only in collectible art which has no substance of artistic merit that can be judged on its own, not by the name, for the benefit of collectors. Not that it is difficult to judge collectible art because of the intrinsic ambiguity in art judgment, for there is no trouble of judgment in uncollectible art, but that it is *impossible* to derive any standard of artistic quality when literally *anything* passes for art if the name—from Leonardos to Warhols—happens to be right for collection purpose. If the name happens to be right, *anything* that he can produce or pretend to produce *as art* will be desired, bought, and collected, no matter what it is that's being produced. All a collector has to say to the world is that he owns a "Picasso," a "Van Gogh," a "Jasper Johns," or whatever name that fits the work in possession.

Of course, the artistic merit of any artwork cannot be determined presently by the current shifts in fortunes and chance. It is a work of history and generations, neither of which can be rushed or manufactured to a lasting result. However, because of its inevitable ties to possession and to the market, collectible art cannot wait for history to judge it; for it has to be collected *now* and by a *living* collector. Nor can it be judged by public acclaim for its survival or extinction; for the public's role in collectible art is fairly negligible. It is instant fame and notoriety for the art and for the collector here and now. No history or public judgment can stand its way.

Chapter 9

Making Instant History

Let's introduce at this point two familiar concepts as a means to clarify and aid our understanding: "Value" and "price." It has been said that a money-hungry man is a man who knows the *price of everything* and the *value of nothing*. This saying defines the terms so simply for us. With the usual caution that all general concepts require, let us look at them further:

Value is for that which we cherish, love, respect, and honor for no other reason than that we are persuaded to feel so. These feelings are normally embodied in ideas, such as Truth, Justice, Beauty, Love, Faith. As ideas they entail little practical or immediate benefit to those dedicated to them, many of whom have died in their defense. Or, these ideas may be found in material objects or concrete human deeds as *symbols* of such ideas. Material objects or concrete human deeds in themselves without their symbolic association with value-ideas are generally regarded as an ephemeral phenomenon unworthy of historical consideration.

Price is for that which we desire, covet, possess, or use for utilitarian and rational reasons with immediate results in view. They are always "things" or something that can be exchanged for things. Hence, all things of price are *interchangeable* within the laws of demand and supply. In other words, things with a price indicating their worth can be exchanged for things that are of comparable worth. The place where this exchange takes place is called the "market." Unlike ideas of value, however, things of price cannot call upon people to die for them. Even as a man works hard to make money, he would certainly not die in defense or dedication of it, for no amount of money would be worth his own life.

Value can be neither established nor attained overnight, not even in one generation. It is the ceaseless work of many generations in history. No ideas of value are ever rationally debated, argued, and voted on, unlike what we would find in Congress or a student body government. Nor are they ever negotiated between two interested parties. For these and other similar reasons that are more a matter of the heart, the ideas of one generation are often considered irrational and face the negligence of later more rationally-minded generations. But what survives is so deeply embedded in our subconscious that we act in everyday life without consciously thinking about such origins of our value.

Price, on the other hand, is debated, argued over, negotiated, and haggled about in *every* instance. Every item on the market that bears a price is subject to the enormously complicated processes of price-jockeying. The price-tag represents the final form such processes ultimately take. The marketplace represents the repository of such price-jocking, to which all things priced are subjected. Hence, every price is determined in the present, here and now. Yesterday's price has no bearing upon today's, nor can tomorrow's price be deducted from today's. In price determination, every day, every moment is a new day and new moment, all without history and sentiments. Every price is real only at the moment the buyer pays, for there is absolutely no reference to anything else. Every price, unlike value, therefore, exists only for the moment.

Value and price, so considered, are almost always diametrically opposed to each other. An idea of truly high value is often low-priced or has no exchangeable price at all. What is high-priced in the marketplace, on the other hand, has little or no true value, although it may be popularly sought after at the moment. In sum, we may safely assume that what is valuable is price-less, and what is highly-priced is value-less. In every society and era, what is historically highly-valued and what is economically highly-priced are in constant struggle to retain or dominate the thoughts and actions of its men, women, and children. It is the eternal conflict symbolizing the conflict between good and evil, soul and body, salvation and damnation, altruism and egotism in every human soul and in every human society.

If we are to take seriously those who profess their love of art, art undoubtedly represents "value," for it is said to be "priceless." But if we are to take seriously what we *know* about the art market, art cannot be anything except a thing with a definite price, subject to all sorts of market consideration. How are we to understand this tangled confusion of value and price of art? Isn't it true that we value art and consider it above money? But, isn't it also true that, as we have seen, art is money and money possesses art?

This confusion can be easily resolved if we fall back on the distinction between the two kinds of art: Collectible and uncollectible. In this scheme, uncollectible art represents value, while collectible art represents price. Nothing in uncollectible art—in literature, music, drama, philosophy—is ever established overnight or instantly priced at the marketplace. All uncollectible art requires the ceaseless work of history and many generations to be established as the embodiment of an idea or a set of related ideas. Shakespeare, Beethoven, Stendhal, and Plato's works—to again mention them as representatives of uncollectible art—are historically established artworks and their "value" is beyond question. Yet, their price at the marketplace is negligible. Copies of their artworks are available for only a few dollars, while such cheap copies by no means lessen their artistic value. It is a rarity that an uncollectible artwork ever becomes involved in the market process of money, price, and possession. It so transpires that in uncollectible art the pleasure is intrinsic to artistic pleasure itself: No investment, no exchangeability, no possession, no denial to others. It is pure art and nothing else.

In collectible art, however, price is everything that art is, and art is everything its price is. A collectible artwork—say, a painting—is said to be "valuable" only in the sense that its "price" is high, for there is no *other way* of knowing the historical value of the artwork. Not only can true "artistic" value not be derived from the specific artwork itself—what can you derive from an "empty canvas" or anything that can be so easily imitated to the tune of half-real and half-forged?—, the market process that requires price-determination here and now allows no historical or generational force to come into play. Often, the art world misuses the term value for price as if they were one and the same. Robert Wraight, for example, says that the collector "doesn't know the value of the painting until he offers it for sale." Love, respect, and honor in collectible art must sooner or later translate into a price that is lovable, respectable, and honorable. When a collector confesses that he "values" art highly, he is talking about those artworks that fetch high prices. The value of art to a collector in collectible art is ALWAYS EQUAL TO ITS PRICE. (We shall explore this theme, in view of its importance, again a little later.)

When art is thus transformed into price, to be defined here and now without the long waiting for history, two phenomena become immediately noticeable, one relating to art and the other to the collector. The first is the instant art-judgment in auction, and the second the conferring of "instant culture" to the collector.

Auctioning, more than any other factor, epitomizes the workings of the market whereby the law of demand and supply creates an instant result, namely, the price. Through the process of bidding and outbidding for an object, the price is determined instantaneously and on the spot. No argument, no debate, no second guessing is allowed in auctioning. Once you put an object on the auction block, or buy one from it, the decision is final and irrevocable. It is the most brutally efficient and unsentimentally rational way of getting things done known to mankind. Its practice is most commonly observed, hence, in the most rational of times and societies—in contemporary West where the market has been prominent for quite some time.

Naturally, then, all things to be auctioned off are items that are of high utility in terms of usefulness and high rationality in terms of profitability. All sorts of merchandise change hands through auctioning. Gems, slaves, professional athletes, collectible art, and any number of other things that are on the market can be auctioned off without sentiment. No one who participates in auctioning approaches it burdened with historical value or human sentiment. Everything on the auction block is just a commodity to be sold to the highest bidder. Auction-goers must be prepared to win or lose with equal poise and equanimity. There is neither reverence, affection, nor respect for the things that are auctioned off. It is the most cool-headed, cold-hearted moment of decision anyone ever faces in his life. Thus, auction, as graphically represented in the stock market, is the essence, the microcosm, the frozen moment symbol of market mechanism.

In the world of collectible art, more and more art buying and selling is done through the auction houses (such as Sotheby's and Christie's), and less and less with the traditional art dealers. In these auction houses is made the instant judgment of artistic worth. Under the auctioneer's gavel, past and present converge to create instant art history. As bids are made, an unknown artwork can emerge as a great work of art, making its author a great artist; as bids are withheld, a famous artwork can fall to humiliation, transforming its hitherto great fame into obscurity.

More often, the auction house is a theatre for spectacles. The size of the price persuaded out of the buyer overshadows the purchased artwork itself as a spectacle. When an artwork is sold at an auction for millions of dollars, it is difficult to look at the work strictly as an artwork without being overwhelmed by the price it commanded. Indeed it would be asking for a miracle to expect people to look at Van Gogh's "Irises" without being reminded of its price of 50,000,000 dollars, completely overshadowing the picture. In fact, it was precisely the size of the price that put the painting in the news. Our modern world demands instantaneous action in virtually every facet of life, including art judgment. Auction has become the modern world's answer to instant art judgment so that it can bypass the cumbersome process of history and generations. For bidding at an auction makes instant history.

Now about the art collector. Art acquisition in America is a relatively recent game. It used to be strictly a European phenomenon until the postwar affluence when Americans began to consider art as a means of investment and a status symbol for the new, idle rich.

As we noted, there are two kinds of art collectors: Amateur collectors and investment collectors. For reasons of investment, profit, and market fluctuations, the investment collector tends to approach the art business with a fairly rational frame of mind. While being the target of criticism for using noble art for his crass capitalism—which incidentally he richly deserves—the investment collector is a fairly uninteresting figure. He is too sane in the business sense, not noticeably susceptible to the melancholia of the art possession. While a crass venture-capitalist of the most contemptible kind, he is not obsessed with art other than for its investment opportunity. To him, art is no different from ordinary stocks, bonds, and real estate. He displays none of the strange, bizarre, and often pathological behavior common to the amateur collector who is our main focus.

It is, then, the amateur collector who collects art for status and other similar psychological reasons, who is the subject of our investigation. The American amateur collector typically is a person of the new-rich leisure class, who requires much justification in the way of his wealth and place in society. None of the idle rich in America, by virtue of its short history of capitalism, is a long-standing family. Being new to the scene, the new rich are constantly in the act of proving their worth, befitting the size of their bank account. Proportional to the size of their wealth, they feel the need to demonstrate that, above all, they are *cultured*.

Since, obviously, they are not cultured, for money-making and cultural pursuit are quite alien to each other, they need some proof of culture in a hurry. In other words, they need *instant culture*. Naturally, collectible art comes to the rescue, for nothing is as handy as art collection for establishing one's instant credit as a cultured elite. By owning a sizable collection of this artist or that—generally well known for his fidelity to trend more than anything else—who has good name-recognition value. Just by purchasing popularly-known but exclusively-priced artworks at auctions, helped by art experts, the new rich gets his name circulated among the art elites of society and acquires the cultural credibility he desperately craves. Sometimes he donates some of his collections to a large university, always a good gesture for instant culture, or loans them for public displays, which establishes him also as a man of charity as well.

Thus, for a few million dollars the new rich can acquire instant cultural recognition that would be impossible in any other way. The man may remain just as stupid, ignorant, or philistine regarding art as before, but his new reputation as an art owner nullifies the old image, giving him instant recognition as a man of taste and culture. This is more true among the new rich, but is also common among the older families as well, such as the Mellons, the Rockefellers, and other less-endowed. In Europe, art ownership is confirmed by the status of the owner, for the upper class are *expected* to own a few precious paintings as a matter of family tradition. In America, in contrast, the status of the owner is confirmed by art ownership.

Typical among the new rich who sought to enhance their culture by instant art ownership, thereby becoming the textbook example of pathological art collection, is a Texas oil millionaire named Algur Meadows (as told mainly by Lawrence Jeppson and Clifford Irving in their respective books on art forgery). Mr. Meadows, while building his fortunes, lived by the motto: "Negotiate the very best possible price when you buy; second, negotiate the easiest terms for payment; and after that negotiate the lowest interest rate." This business principle served him well in his fortune-building but, when applied to his culture-building, turned out to be a cause of misfortune. Feeling the keen need of instant culture, Mr. Meadows predictably turned to art collection, following the advice of art experts. But in his pursuit of culture, he was still the bargain-hunter he had always been, for he sought to buy the artworks at the "lowest possible price." By buying up many well known names for his collections, Mr. Meadows, hitherto a merely unknown money-monger, suddenly gained his respectability as an art collector and therefore as a cultured man. As part of his image-making, he donated many artworks to the Southern Methodist University. Unfortunately, however, practically all of his artworks that he had bargained so hard for, including the SMU collections, turned out to be forgeries. More than his art collections, this act of foolishness—for he dared to announce his forgeries publicly by going after the culprits, namely, Elmyr de Hory and company who sold him the fake works en masse—immortalized Algur Meadows in the annals of the delicate art game and instant culture.

The psychology of instant culture reveals a trait that is strongly associated with money. People with the idea that money can buy anything or everyone has his price tend to think that anything is possible if the right amount of money is applied. In most cases, of course, they are right, for money can indeed buy almost anything if the amount is right, and virtually everyone does have a price for his body and soul. This does not necessarily reflect poorly on human nature or the evil of money. It merely reveals the psychology of a money-centered society where nothing else is used to measure moral values or behavioral proprieties.

Along with art collection as a means of acquiring instant culture and as a short-cut to demonstrating nobility of heart and loftiness of purpose, we can mention three more things in society where money may be used to bypass time and effort.

First, there is "instant salvation" whereby a wealthy man can donate an appropriate amount of money to a church of his choice to be assured of his immortality and salvation. No religious institution would deny a man's entry into the ranks of the saved when he donates sufficient funds for the things the church deems necessary, such as adding a new wing, renovating the sanctuary, installing a new stereo system, or putting in a new kitchen. This way the man need not demonstrate his salvation in actual, and very often uncomfortable, deed; all he has to do is write out the check for the proper amount.

Second, there is "instant love" whereby, in exchange, a man pays the object of his fancy an appropriate amount of money in appreciation. This may be done in an outright fashion, such as prostitution, or it may be done in a more discreet manner, such as buying jewelry, inviting to a weekend on a yacht, offering an attractive salary. The end-result is still the same: The man gets the "love" of a woman. All he has to do is become a man of wealth or of power to put it into effect. What he gets may be instant, superficial love, also instantly dissolvable when the effect wears off. But he is satisfied with it and wishes for nothing else.

Third, close to instant culture, there is "instant education" whereby a wealthy man can donate funds for appropriate items to a university— a new stadium, a new art collection as in Meadows's case, a new lab, a new library, whatever. In return, the university will confer upon him an honorary doctorate. Even the stupidest, most ignorant, most uncultured man can gain instant respectability when his name appears after the title of "Doctor." Never mind that he has always loathed books, learning, and intellectualism, for, as John Kenneth Galbraith said in another context, wealth *is* always the greatest enemy of learning. All that can be instantly forgotten upon the presentation of his check.

We now see that the psychology of art collection is fairly complex. As we noted, the *negative* factor of art collection, stronger than the positive in the mind of the collector acts as his motive, denying the others the enjoyment of the artwork in his possession. But what is indeed the *positive* factor that drives a person to art collection and possession, since money is not the object? What kind of pleasure does the collector ultimately derive from his collections? How does the idea of instant culture—along with instant salvation, instant love, and instant education—compel the collector toward his insatiable desire to collect and possess? What indeed is it all for?

We shall turn to these questions next.

Chapter 10

The Pleasure Factor

There are three distinct types of worth that every artwork brings forth to the world. The first has to do with uncollectible art; the second with the art market; and the third with the collector. Let's look at each of them more closely.

We may speak of the first one as representing "artistic value" which, as noted earlier, is determined chiefly by history and public appreciation. This artistic value in our present context is observed almost exclusively in uncollectible art. Correspondingly, an uncollectible artwork's market value—as opposed to artistic value—is almost totally negligible. "Romeo and Juliet" or "the Fifth Symphony," for example, is available at a ticket price of a few dollars. This does not mean, of course, that there is no cost involved in the continuing presentation of uncollectible art, for it has to be staged, performed, or printed. How large is the cost— not price or value—for staging, performing, and printing a work of uncollectible art? We can only guess. If all the production costs of performances and printed copies for "Romeo and Juliet" in history were combined, they would perhaps approach in the billions. The sale of recordings for Beethoven's "Ninth" alone amounts to many millions of dollars annually. Considering this, even the most expensive painting in the world would amount to no more than a fraction of these uncollectible artworks. In this sense, the "artistic value" we speak of in uncollectible art is not entirely without concrete justification for being historically valued, if in fact such a crude demonstration is necessary to show that uncollectible art costs money too. Then why is uncollectible art generally thought of as having no market value? The reason for the view is that the market price associated with the uncollectible works is so *spread out* among the art-loving public that it is almost as if these artworks were *free* to the public, and in some cases they *are*. Rarely is an uncollectible art staged, performed or printed as a money-making venture.

Compare this fact with the auctioneer's gavel that announces millions of dollars for this one painting or that, which appears spectacularly expensive and awesome in its implied artistic value. The world associates the collectible artwork with this great singular price and, therefore, its imputed artistic value. The higher the price, the greater its artistic value. But the truth is quite different. We now know that the market price is wholly unrelated to the work's artistic value; neither is the price itself. While seemingly spectacular and awesome, the latter is a small one compared to the cumulative expenses in historical presentations of famous uncollectible works. Besides, no collectible art has ever been subjected to historical and public appreciation for its pure artistic value *without* being overshadowed by other factors, such as money, price, possession. Thus, in spite of the fact that we routinely assign prices to it, it is impossible to assess what a collectible work's true artistic value might be.

We may find the second kind of worth in "economic price" that an artwork, as a commodity, can command at the marketplace. All collectible art falls under this category. This is the kind of value that investor-collectors are thinking of when they talk about the joy of art-collection. The worth of each artwork is classified by its putative market price under a normal competitive (auction) circumstance. According to this scheme of classification, a work that fetches a high price is "high art," a middle price "middle art," and a low price "low art," since no other way of judging their value is possible in collectible art. The market, however, claims that an artwork's economic price *contains*, or is *derived* from, its artistic value. Its rationale is that the market price of the "Irises" at 50 million dollars contains or is derived from its "artistic value" that history has conferred upon it. A high price on a artwork is thus deemed equal to its artistic value.

Of course, this argument is patently false. We have, as noted, no way of knowing what the work's "artistic value" might be, since it has not been subjected to pure historical judgment. The "Irises," like all other collectibles, has been on the market ever since its production. Its "history" is none other than the history of its market price. The only way we may be able to guess its historical place is, in the fashion of "Romeo and Juliet" or the "Fifth," would be to see, as a way of its historical assessment, how many people take a special trip to a museum or an exhibition *specifically* to see the painting or how much it costs to maintain its exhibition, and so on. But, just now, that calculation is useless, for, even if the "Irises" were available for public viewing, people would more likely be motivated to see the painting because it *costs* such a huge sum, not just to appreciate the painting for itself. The "Irises" is a celebrity because of its cost, not for its intrinsic artistic value. Besides, how many people would *repeat*, as they do with "Romeo and Juliet" or the "Fifth," their viewing of the "Irises" over and over again?

We may speak of the third kind of worth as the "pleasure factor," which is mainly associated with art collection. The pleasure factor is often claimed to derive from the two elements discussed above, namely, "artistic value" and "market price." What gives the particular artwork its distinct pleasure, the collector may argue, is its historical acclaim to fame and its corresponding market price that fits the fame. But we know from our previous discussions that this claim is false for these three simple reasons.

First, there is no great pleasure derived from looking at an artwork that is supposedly intrinsic to all art-looking. Solely on the basis of what one sees from the canvas, if we may be frank about it and not be fearful of our supposed ignorance about art, there is really nothing that is so terribly wonderful about any art, classic or modern. "You cannot *do* anything with a work of art," Lawrence Jeppson quotes Hilton Kramer's article in *The New York Times*. "You can only stand there. The action, clearly, is elsewhere." Where? Kramer's answer: In hype and money. Or, we might add, in one's pure imagination helped by the hype and money. The kind of "thrills" and "wonders" of paintings that some neurotically-inclined art-lovers describe are quite alien to the reaction of most people who may otherwise be intelligent and sensitive in matters of creativity. They may also have been derived from sources other than from the artworks themselves, for such psychidelic reactions can be self-induced either from their own imagination or from their subconsciously pre-programmed reaction to art. What could possibly be the intrinsic pleasure found in looking at an aristocratic face or a Biblical scene in a classic picture, or a set of rectangles, triangles, circles and lines, and sometimes not even those things, as in modern painting? Besides, as likely as not, any of them could very well be a forgery, the one fact that instantaneously cools their ardently confessed love for the artwork, thus baring their shallowness, hypocrisy, and romantic self-delusions. Those who genuinely claim something thrilling and wonderful from paintings, beyond the cursory desire to buy one for a few bucks to cover a wall, are likely to be either self-convincing liars or the neurotically deluded types.

Second, art collectors as a rule know next to nothing about art, much less about artistic value aside from its market price and hyped celebrity. It would be laughable to think of the late Nelson Rockefeller, one of the biggest art collectors in recent memory, as an art connoisseur, a man driven by his love of art. The aforementioned Mr. Meadows may be extreme, but people who collect art for possession, not for purely economic reasons, are not that different from the basic mold of Rockefellers and Meadows. Since they are basically art-and culture-illiterate, they must rely on experts to help them in choosing well known artists and popular artworks. Like a blind person without a seeing-eye dog, these collectors would be completely lost without expert guidance in matters of art. Besides, if they loved art as a thing of beauty, they might enjoy sunsets, clouds, flowers, and any number of other very beautiful but inexpensive things, not just the beautiful things that cost a lot. Also, as lovers of art they might want to spread it around to others, not just keep it to themselves, as a natural gesture for things they truly value and love, like the rest of us who love things of beauty but do not collect them, much less for an astronomical sum of money. What does a true lover of art do, except enjoy its pleasure and share it with as many people as possible? It is difficult to imagine that Rockefellers and Meadows are capable of doing either.

Third, these collectors whose interest is mainly in possession and status-satisfaction are not strenuously interested in making money through art dealing. They have too much money already—which is what compels them to go into art collection in the first place—and, in the second place, they don't seriously consider art to be a good source of money-making. It is only those middling-capitalists with a lot of pecuniary desires yet with little capital in hand, certainly no big name millionaires, who consider art a possible business venture. Indeed, if the big time collectors were interested in the market comings and goings of profit-making in art, they would find something else—oil, defense contract, foreign loan, for example—to be more profitable. Art may appreciate spectacularly, but it can depreciate just as unpredictably also, and is simply too few in number to be a source of purely economic consideration. Very few of their accountants and investment experts would recommend art strictly as business ventures.

Then, of course, there is always the "negative pleasure" we spoke of earlier, the pleasure of denying other people—especially competing collectors with equally large sums of money to spend on art—from owning or enjoying the work in one's own possession. Psychologists might argue that this principle of negative pleasure is just as strong, or stronger, in pushing the collector into art possession. There is much truth in this. A youth gang member might "conquer" a girl who is desired by all other gang members even though she is not particularly desirable to him, just to deny the other gang members the pleasure of her company. But this may not be enough to explain the collector's obsessive and often bizarre behavior concerning art possession. The "pleasure factor" we speak of here must contain something more than the "negative pleasure" of denying others access to what one owns.

Is there another source of "pleasure" that could explain art possessiveness? I think there is, and I would, for want of a better term, call it the "Dictatorial Pleasure" factor. What could this dictatorial pleasure factor be?

To put it simply: Dictatorial pleasure refers to all elements of psychic satisfaction—from extreme pleasure to extreme displeasure, utilitarian-rational pleasure falling somewhere in between the two extremes—associated with what is *bought* by money. A person buys something for many different reasons. But whatever reasons he may have for spending a certain amount of money, the pleasure he derives from what he has bought can be thus expressed, at least in the art collection business, as dictatorial pleasure. Let me elaborate, especially in relation to art collection as explainable by this factor, on why I have called such pleasure dictatorial pleasure.

First is the obvious economic fact. Even without help from a professional economist, any reasonable person knows that in a market society the pleasure associated with commodity X is precisely equal to the *price* paid for X. Nothing more, nothing less. The pleasure, whatever it is, however strong or weak it may be, cannot be measured greater or smaller than the price one has voluntarily paid for it. There are bargains, of course, or some unfair advantage one might take in getting the bargain, that may distort this balance somewhat. But even the definition of what constitutes a "bargain" can vary, not depending on the amount of money paid toward the price, but depending on the unreliable psychology of the buyer who thinks anything is a bargain if he likes the commodity well enough. In all this transaction, the commanding psychology in dictatorial pleasure is that all things can be *converted* into the dictates of market price. This rule enormously simplifies the economic ways of the market and the dictatorial mind of the buyer: Money is everything and more money is more of everything.

The art collector, now in full control of his collections, need not trouble himself with this or that aspect of art, for all he has to show is how much money is represented by his collections. If he paid 50 million dollars for a Van Gogh, the pleasure he expects to get out of it is precisely equal to that amount (unless the price has appreciated since he bought it). It is money pleasure to be sure, but in the dictates of market price there is no other way of defining pleasure, of course in the strict economic sense. Looking at it strictly from the economic point of view, the pleasure one gets from his collections is really no different from the pleasure one gets from other commodities, the amount of pleasure varying in proportion to the price he paid. This may range from the small pleasure of having bought a good lunch to the big pleasure of having bought a Van Gogh. But still the pleasure corresponds to the price, nothing else.

However, what is most significant to our understanding of the compelling force behind art possessiveness, aside from the money factor, is the hidden psychological factor expressed in art possession. Since there is neither the utilitarian-rational factor of art collection—for there is no functional use for art, and profit-making is not the main motive for collectors—, nor what might be called "love for art"—for they know nothing about art, and cannot find anything lovable enough in painting to the tune of millions of dollars to pay for one—in art collection, we still have to look for the hidden motive within the dictatorial pleasure of what money can do.

Let's rephrase the point. If there is no inherently functional purpose (either in usefulness or in profit-making), and there is no explainable source of love (for collectors are both philistines toward artistic life and incapable of loving anything or anybody by virtue of their class and money), why would the collector spend such enormous sums of money on useless and unlovable objects? After all possible factors have been considered, the only answer that remains unalterable is that the collector feels he can turn his nose up on everyone by demonstrating that he can *buy* up the most *precious* heritage of mankind into his personal possession. HE IS BUYING AND OWNING A PART OF HUMAN HISTORY! While he, and a large segment of the public, may be playing along the game of philanthropy, of being the curator of human culture, of do-gooding, the simple truth is that the collector displays profound contempt toward mankind and its most valued legacy, namely, art. Such contempt has been demonstrated only by the most despicable and powerful of dictators in the past and present.

In what more triumphant way can a man of money—the most pursued yet most despised of all things in life—show his contempt for mankind's most cherished treasures and demonstrate his hatred for mankind itself using his money other than by depriving others of their most cherished treasures? If mankind thought of love as its most cherished emotion and it could be somehow "collected" with money, the collector would have lost no time collecting and possessing mankind's most treasured love-emotions into his own private collections. In what more convincing a way can the wealthy man, superficially admired but deeply hated, and always insecure with his place in the public mind, steal the most important of human creation yet still glory in the name of good will, philanthropy, and love of art?

What is called "art" is a universal human possession, belonging exclusively neither to a nation nor to an individual. No nation on earth, whatever its political or religious persuasion, which happens to be a temporary curator of its own share of art, would wholly deny other nations the same pleasure of enjoying its art. Yet, once fallen into the private hands of collectors, it is as good as nonexistent. Art simply vanishes from the view of mankind into private collections. It is as clear as daylight, then, that every artwork "collected" by a collector is art lost to the public who rightly is entitled to all its past heritage bequeathed to it by history. But why is every artwork sold to a private collection so *celebrated* in the media and by the public as an instance of art-loving, not lamented or causing outrage? Why is there no cry of thievery whenever an artwork is collected into private possession and is so hugely celebrated among art-people who, as dealers, experts, and artists, share in the profit of it? (The only answer I can think of, aside from our acceptance of money-dictatorship in society, is that in spite of all that media hype and price, people don't think collectible art is *that* important. So, what's in a Van Gogh or a Jackson Pollock as art that is so important? Compare this with a hypothetical government edict that forbids any future performances of Shakespeare's plays or Beethoven's symphonies. For the latter, there would be such a public outrage that the government would perhaps fall.)

Let's follow a typical collector who has just paid five million dollars for a Rembrandt and retired to his private study to look at the painting placed in the corner of the room. He is satisfied with his new collection, smiling profusely for a few minutes. But what is he *really* thinking? About the artwork? Not likely, for he knows practically nothing about art, not enough to pay that much money for it anyway. About the artist? Hardly, for he knows far less about him than about the artwork, and cares the least about him as a person. About the price? Perhaps, thinking he could have bid a little lower, maybe he was too jumpy with his own bid, but it's all done now, no use second-guessing. No, none of these things occupies his mind very long. Yet he feels immensely satisfied. What kind of satisfaction is this? Why, none other than the satisfaction of a dictator who has vanquished all his opponents in order to own and dictate his part of history, except in this case it was his money that did the job. It is the wealthy man's revenge for being unloved, the display of his immense contempt for mankind, his demonstration of what money can do, and the final triumph of money over art when he puts the painting in his vault and locks it. Now, history's treasure, the world's object of love, and mankind's living legacy has forever fallen into his private domain, and only he holds the key.

When a collector owns an artwork, he owns *all* of the artwork—the artist's whole creative output, the world's whole historical record of it, mankind's whole memory of the work. Nothing of the original work remains once it is collected into the vault of a man's private possession, only its fading memories and in fragments. Theoretically as well as practically, *all* of Van Gogh—for that matter, *all* of all known artists—can be the possession of one single man if he has enough money to buy *all* of the works. The idea of *owning* all of Van Gogh, all of Michelangelo, all of Picasso, all of anyone who is anybody in art, is so spine-tingling that its excitement can easily equal that of the most possessive materialist, the most tyrannical tyrant, and the most dictatorial dictator in human history. All this is done, mind you, under the glare of media fanfare and of public boasting and adulation.

Shouldn't this be enough to inspire the collector, a man of enormous wealth but of nothing else, to COLLECT AND POSSESS ALL THE ARTWORKS IN THE WORLD IF HE COULD?

There is another side yet to the psychology of dictatorial pleasure. A man who *has to* pay money for something that he has no immediate use for tends to develop a strong sense of contempt and hatred toward, and even the desire to torture, what he has to *buy*. Since he is compelled to buy the artwork neither for use nor for love, his only source of satisfaction is in the fact that other people, who may cherish it, cannot have the pleasure of enjoying it. But for that, he has just paid millions. The thing is loved by everyone, but he cannot see any clear value in or derive pleasure from it for his lack of knowledge or ability, or whatever. Then, what is he supposed to feel toward the thing but contempt, hatred, and a desire to play with it? The only thing a man with money respects is someone or something that his money *cannot* buy. But he wants to *buy* everything that he desires, or even respects, only to feel still unloved and still hateful toward it. Hence that terrible dilemma of his inability to love what he buys.

The interplay between money-love and money-hate is a fascinating one. It is not unlike a John who pays for a prostitute's service he deems desirable yet feels compelled to hate her and her service at the same time. There is no way love can be bought and still be true; there is no way art can be bought and still be loved, respected, and honored. What does a man feel once he *owns* the prostitute? What is the burning desire in him to do with what he has *paid for?* The profound sense of triumph over everyone who can't have it any more, the inevitable contempt for what can be bought with money, the satisfaction of a conquest and ownership over what mankind reveres, now in his sole possession, is so great that even the strongest of drugs cannot be comparable with the collector's dictatorial pleasure that compels him yet toward another acquisition.

Now, in all these workings of the collector's mind, that he is buying "works of art" is entirely secondary, a fact only marginally alive in his subconsciousness. Anything that is recommended by experts, is talked about in the media, is popular to the public, will do for his collections. Not unlike the drug market, then, the art market has arisen to meet this addictive quality in art possession. It is not what "art" is collected and possessed, but that something is collected and possessed *as* art that counts.

Since no one really knows what art is, what "real art" looks like next to "non-real art," the art market has risen to the occasion and has been pushing anything-as-art, selling illusion to the insatiable but essentially stupid art collector, a member of what Robert Wraight calls the "Idiot Brigade" of art collectors. In a world where real and unreal coexist side by side, where mystery only increases its market price, what passes for art and sold into famous collections is often nothing more than a canvas suitably framed, displayed, and hyped as art.

This phantom art, the art that cannot possibly exist in a more rational reality and in a more reasonable frame of mind, that nevertheless *does* exist to form great art fortunes and collections, then, is the subject to which we will now turn.

Chapter 11

The Art That Never Is

Some of us might be surprised at this, but art is actually *made*, not created. What an artist creates—or more often what he *doesn't* create—makes little difference. Art is made where the artwork is, in Hilton Kramer's description, "talked about, reproduced, debated, exalted, sold, and—best of all—exposed." Or, in short, hyped—not unlike the "art auctions" of the late Andy Warhol's collections which were charitably described as "some sort of sick joke" and "awful junk" by some participants.

After all the hustle and bustle of art-making activity at the marketplace, the *artwork* itself often turns out, according to Kramer, to be a "distinct disappointment." In spite of the artwork's market price being equal to the pleasure it brings to the collector, the hypothetical collector mentioned in the preceding chapter might feel, while staring at the painting that just cost him millions of dollars, the inevitable pangs of disappointment. It is not unlike the bridegroom who had ardently courted and finally wed the most sought after girl in the village who might think the next day, Is this all there is? A similar thought might creep into the collector's dubiously pleased subconsciousness.

After all, no artwork sold and bought on the market can ever equal in value its hype and resulting price accorded it. The hype is staged, the purchase dynamic, the anticipation exciting. But the artwork itself is one-dimensional, stationary, and unchanging. Moreover, very few things in life live up to their anticipated billing. This art-making through hype, as with the "name factor," is a classic case of form making substance or the package overriding what's inside.

Granted, this hype is a fact of life in a market society where every commodity must be packaged and sold against tough competition. But a question nags on our mind nevertheless: Why does this rule of hype apply ONLY TO COLLECTIBLE ART, AND NOT UNCOLLECT-IBLE ART? There is virtually no staged hype on Shakespeare or Beethoven, or even on other lesser artists in drama, music, literature, philosophy, whatever. Almost never does an uncollectible artwork of inconsequential importance ever gain entry into the art Hall of Fame by being "talked about, reproduced, debated, exalted, sold, and—best of all—exposed"?

There are two answers to this question, neither of which pleases us very much.

First, we can say that what passes for art in collectible art is *not* really art, it is a common market-commodity like tooth paste or a dime novel that must be packaged and pushed. If it *were* real art, why would it need all the mechanisms of commercial hype, which, in the case of uncollectibles, only history and generational judgment could perform?

Second, we can also say that there is no such thing as (collectible) art that can be defined as a *material reality*. Since "art" can range from the most elaborate and overwhelming presence—say, Michelangelo's fresco on the ceiling of the Sistine Chapel—to the bare, empty canvas merely displayed with a frame around it—say, Jo Baer's "Grayed Yellow Vertical Rectangle"—, and all the varieties of arrangement and expression in between, this answer demands a serious hearing.

On second thought, however, we realize that these two answers are really the flip-side of *each other*, the first fact being necessitated by the second and the second fact requiring the first. It makes perfect sense. If a snake oil salesman wants to sell his wares as a cure-all, since it may or may not cure anything at all, he has to rely almost exclusively on his extraordinary skill as a salesman—crowd-pleasing, dynamic, believable, well-staged and delivered, and appearing sincere by appealing to some higher virtues. In short, all the skills of modern commercial hype.

If, by the same token, an art dealer wants to sell a painting which, by itself, is not any more aesthetically pleasing than a beautiful sunset or a flower, or is not any more comprehensible than a scratch mark on the wall made by his two-year old grandson, he will *have to* rely on his commercial hyping skills to call upon a loftier and certainly more practical virtue called "art," "love of art," "art collection," and so on. Reflecting on this line of thought I think we are on the right track and one step closer to unraveling the many layers in the mysteries of art.

There is no law that says what art should be. But there is law that says what is *not* art, meaning forgeries. Consider the two contradictions in the following two cases.

No matter how beautiful, how aesthetically pleasing, or close to the supposed original, a forgery is considered in the art establishment to be nonexistent, a nonentity, a zero-value item, and law—being inherently friendly toward the establishment—is fairly harsh on this. For example, two versions of Leonardo's "La Belle Ferronniere," the portrait of a lady of his days, appeared on the scene, one in the Louvre in France and the other in Kansas City which was put on sale. Obviously both were old pictures and very similar in appearance, which most people, including art experts, could not tell apart. Now, a controversy arose when a world authority in art—a Sir Joseph Duveen, a rather big name in art business—called the latter a forgery, and the Kansas City owner sued him in protest. The question that had to be settled was: Which is the *real* "La Belle Ferronniere"? Depending on the outcome, one picture would be instantly devalued to nonexistent art, a nonentity, a zero-value item, and the other would remain on the highest pedestal in the art world. In view of the similarities in appearance and age of the two versions, experts gave contradictory opinions in the courtroom. Worn out by time and expense, the case was eventually settled between the parties out of court, but the real question still remained unanswered. The Kansas City Leonardo had come very close to being declared by law to be *no art*, a nothing, although some experts were on its side as real art.

On the other hand, law is extremely lenient toward nonexistent art. A nonentity, a zero-value item (in short, anything-as-art) will pass for art if it is promoted and sold *as art* by the establishment. If a dealer promotes and sells a blank canvas, a Black-and-Decker shovel, or any other such nothings, properly framed, catalogued, and displayed as art at a huge price, no law will call it a blatant fraud, an obvious con job, or a simple sham. (This has happened as a matter of fact, the shovel being an "artwork" titled "In Advance of the Broken Arm" by pop artist Marcel Duchamp whose plain urinal, but signed by him as his "artwork," is really his most famous work, now prominently displayed at the Yale University Art Gallery.) If law defines and punishes forgeries as no art, why can it *not* define and punish art that *is* no art? If an empty canvas— which to our commonsense understanding is obviously *nothing*, and certainly no art if we believe art or anything else offered as a commodity must be *something*—is sold as art, should it not be considered a fraud, punishable by law?

If a diamond dealer sold a common rock as a diamond, the seller would obviously be breaking a law. If nothing is sold as something, even in art, would it not be a violation of some law? How can a nothing be promoted and sold as something? Apparently it is possible in art. But why? Why is this silence of conspiracy, why is this ignorance of the most obvious fraud, why is this acceptance of the most blatant violation to commonsense and reason?

The answer, although it takes some mental acrobatics to comprehend and its implication is fairly mind-boggling, is simple: BECAUSE ART *IS* NOTHING. No one in the art establishment, no law-enforcement agency, no art-loving public, none, has ever declared this as public knowledge, but it has been so *in practice*. Whether openly acknowledged or not, it has been a universal secret in reality, that *art is nothing*. Or to put it in another way, *art doesn't have to be anything in particular to pass for art*. Like snake oil for cure-all, anything can pass for art if one can promote it and sell it to the nearest collector who is appropriately wealthy, stupid, and possessive, three essential qualifications for a classic sucker in the P.T. Barnum mold. But unlike snake oil, ours goes by the noble name of "art," not high comedy or practical joke as it probably should. From this vantage point, the only difference between real art and no art is determined by which side the law stands on—a fairly negligible yardstick with which to judge, of all things, art.

It is only in the world of art and art collection that this acquiescence to nonsense reigns supreme as a matter of daily routine. In a real world in which everyone knows the earth is round, the art world is still thought flat, and more strangely, this misknowledge brings about no visible ill-consequences to the believer. The only conclusion possible from this contradiction is to assume that the world in which they live—that is, the art world—must be immune to the distinctions between real and unreal, nothing and something, true and false, and round and flat. As a means of furthering our comprehension, try to switch to uncollectible art and fathom what would happen if incomprehensible notes, scribblings, or babble could pass as music, literature, or philosophy.

In collectible art, an artwork is judged by factors that have nothing to do with the artwork itself. All *external* factors—age, signature, price, collectability—and nothing in the artwork itself, come together to form its value. Obviously, the only reason for that is that there is nothing "intrinsic" to the artwork which can cause it to stand on its own. The empty canvas and the shovel are extreme but by no means exceptional examples. As such, if we removed the external factors—as in the case of uncollectible art—, how much of collectible art could stand on their own as art? Or, how do we explain the fact that two very similar works attributed to Leonardo would undergo a hair-splitting argument in court? If the two versions were close enough to convince some experts that they are both Leonardo's, why does anything else matter? But whether the work *was* by Leonardo, not whether it was *good enough* to be by Leonardo, was the whole point in the dispute. Wouldn't the forged work of Leonardo—whichever turned out to be the forgery—, still good enough to fool everyone for centuries, be a better work of art than the empty canvas or the shovel or the urinal? Such questions have been raised by just about everyone who has had a stake in the art business, but in a way that was simply a reaction of exasperation, not a serious question that threatens to unravel the very legitimacy of the art establishment.

This point brings our quest to a fairly startling hypothesis. What if all the known collectible artworks were destroyed overnight—no more Leonardos, Van Goghs, Picassos, or Pollocks? Surely, it would be devastating to collectors, dealers, experts, and museums. But how would the general public, many of them lovers of beautiful things, react? Just what indeed would their reaction be? I raise this hypothetical question to point out the essential nonexistence, the mirage-like quality of collectible art. Even granted that it is real, why would the public care if these rare works of art that are in the sole possession of some particular man, in some remote museum, is no longer there? More to our point, would the public be terribly upset that the portrait of a lady by Leonardo or the empty canvas by Jo Baer or the shovel by Duchamp (or actually by Black-and-Decker) no longer exists? That Artwork X (1) exists somewhere remote from the familiar; (2) is owned by some wealthy man one only hears about; (3) costs a lot of money one can only fathom; and (4) is called "art," but in truth, does little or nothing to the rest of the world. It is like a great fabulous gem that (1) exists somewhere remote from the familiar; (2) is owned by some wealthy man...

On the other hand, what would happen if plays by Shakespeare or symphonies by Beethoven or dialogues by Plato no longer existed? Wouldn't people miss Shakespeare, Beethoven, or Plato? Of course, collectibles are subject to periodic disappearing acts whenever one is sold to a private collection, with the public hardly missing it. Uncollectibles, on the other hand, can never disappear either as a physical act or as a mental memory.

Now, we have come to a point in our quest where we must confront perhaps the most significant crossroads concerning the realness of collectible art. Two choices of thought and action are open to us: Either we go along with the art establishment and pretend that art is real and wonderful as we are told in spite of all the facts contrary to our reason and commonsense; or go boldly where no man or woman has ever gone before concerning art into the world of sense and logic, guided solely by desire for truth. The first of these two alternatives would be chosen obviously by art-people who are collectors, dealers, experts, artists, curators, and so on whose very livelihood and reason for being are staked in the orthodox, party line version of the art establishment. In spite of the terrible violence this view does to everything that is sane and reasonable, they will not change their views, and we can only wish them well with their continuing prosperity and satisfaction.

For us who have chosen the second alternative, I say, let's get on with our journey toward the land of facts, sanity, and truth. So far, we can say these things about collectible art as incontrovertible:

1.   REAL ART AND UNREAL ART (FORGERIES) ARE INDISTINGUISHABLE. IN OTHER WORDS, THERE IS NO DIFFERENCE BETWEEN WHAT IS REAL AND WHAT IS UNREAL IN COLLECTIBLE ART, AND WHAT IS REAL CAN BE EASILY REPLACED BY WHAT IS UNREAL.

2.   IN COLLECTIBLE ART, EVEN WHAT IS CONSIDERED A REAL ARTWORK CAN BE SOMETHING, NOTHING, OR ANYTHING—AN EMPTY CANVAS, A SHOVEL, A URINAL, OR A CHILD'S SCRATCH ON THE WALL—AS LONG AS IT IS CATALOGUED, FRAMED, DISPLAYED, AND SOLD AS ART.

3.   WHILE IT IS BOTH REAL AND UNREAL, BOTH ANYTHING AND NOTHING, BOTH BEAUTIFUL AND UGLY, WHAT IS UNREAL, NOTHING, AND UGLY CAN ALSO BE SOLD AT A HIGH PRICE ON THE ART MARKET ALONG WITH WHAT IS REAL, SOMETHING, AND BEAUTIFUL.

How is all this contradiction possible? How can the unreal pass for the real, nothing or anything for something, imitation for the real? In other words, how can the round world be thought of as flat? Two answers are possible:

First, it can be perpetuated and believed as *forced truth* in a totalitarian society, in a theocratic community, in a militaristic state, where a certain belief is forced onto everyone through propaganda, upbringing, collective education, or whatever.

Second, (and here is the most difficult step for anyone to take, but courage and truth shall be our guide) it can be perpetuated as an *ELABORATE POPULAR HOAX* in an open, democratic society where everyone is voluntarily persuaded.

In an open, democratic society, contrary to the conventional wisdom, everyone is a sucker for hoax. In a totalitarian, theocratic, or militaristic society, only the government may lie. But in an open, democratic society *everyone* may lie simply because, in the absence of powers-that-be, everyone has to persuade everyone in order to survive. Earning a living in the former society only requires pleasing the powers-that-be, but in the latter society one has to please everyone, for everyone is like everyone else. Hence, hoax is much easier to perpetuate in an open, democratic society than one that is more thoroughly controlled. In an open, democratic society, IF YOU FOOL ONE, YOU CAN FOOL EVERYONE BY USING THE SAME INSTRUMENT OF FOOLING. If the snake oil salesman has a tactic good enough to fool Citizen A, the same tactic can be used to fool Citizens B, C, D, E, F...and Z. That's why television ads in America work so well. In the Soviet Union or in the Amish community, for example, only the affluent, stupid, and possessive (remember? the characteristics of art collectors), a rather small segment in any case, would be foolish enough to be affected by the same ads.

ART AS HOAX.

How could it be possible? The noblest, and most beautiful of all human endeavors as a simple hoax?

On the other hand, how could it *not* be?

Chapter 12

Art, the Art Market, and Market Art

Declaring art an elaborate hoax, even when there is good evidence to say so, requires some further explaining. By way of furnishing that explanation, I should like to further elaborate what I mean by "art" and the "art market," and the somewhat new term "market art" as they are used in this book.

I. Art is the artist's imaginations, thoughts, ideas, or messages that crystallize through the specific art form chosen by the artist as his medium. In collectible art it may appear as a picture or as a sculpture. In uncollectible art it may take the form of a novel, a play, a composition, or a philosophy. What begins as an entirely private endeavor ends up, when completed, in public domain as art. Hence each artwork is nothing but the artist's conception of the world, humanity, and, not infrequently, of himself and art itself. The power of art is as the artist can convey it through his artistic originality, craftsmanship, and intellectual clarity that are at the service of his creative impulse and active mind. However, this creative impulse and active mind belong to the artist, and the artist only, only so long as they remain independent of the market.

II. The art market has everything to do with "market" and little or nothing to do with "art." That the market happens to deal in artworks is purely accidental, for the way the market mechanism operates is wholly independent of art and the artist. Certainly the market *makes* art, where art then becomes a commodity that it sells and buys. Whether or not the art market is helpful to art is a moot question, although mostly detrimental to it, for the art market is there neither to support art nor to help the artist. By its own laws of demand and supply, the art market is first and last a *market* where commodities are sold and bought. Like all other variations of the marketplace, the art market exists for itself as an institution and operates to protect its profit-making.

III. Market art is that part of art that is directly under the market's control or influence. Market art is therefore conceived, produced, and processed in a large measure with the market in mind. It is the peculiar fate of collectible art that it must become market art in order to survive and, in the process, it loses its identity as art and becomes commodity.

In collectible art, it is impossible to separate art and market. On the other hand, uncollectible art is virtually immune to market control or influence. In it, the public—however small a segment—participates directly to determine its survival or prosperity. Market art—typically in painting and sculpture—is inseparable from the market and ultimately becomes its ward, so to speak. Upon becoming market art, or art commodity, little trace of the original purpose can be salvaged in the artwork. As market art, the artwork is to be sold, collected, and possessed like all other market commodities. Once transformed into market art, then, the artwork is subject to the same corrupting mechanisms of the marketplace which spares nothing in its singular existence for profit.

A hoax is a deliberate game of deception, presenting unreality as reality, bad as good, nonexistence as existence. When I speak of art as a hoax, of course, I am referring to the workings of the art market which transform art into market art. The art hoax is created and maintained as THE *PROCESS* IN WHICH THE MARKET TRANSFORMS ART INTO MARKET ART. Market art, whatever its origin as art, no longer owes its existence to any particular artistic design or purpose. Its main design or purpose is dictated now by the market's, not art's. In many instances, of course, the hoax is concocted by artists themselves, not necessarily by the market, as in the case of empty-canvas art, shovel-and-urinal art, and enterprising pop artists. In such instances, art *is* unabashedly conceived by these artists *as* market art, thereby skipping directly to its commodity stage, making no pretenses of their work being art at all.

Often, the process is thought of as being "natural" to the workings of the art world itself, which may be responsible for the public confusion about art, the art market, and market art. The artist may begin as a market artist, that is, one is interested only in producing and selling market art, rather than art from his creative impulse, and give the market all his cooperation. Or, market art, in its corrupt form, may still insist on using the term "art" even when it is sold to the highest bidder and is possessed by the collector with all the contempt that such possession inevitably brings about. The art market, on its part, may partake in many staged activities publicly hyped as philanthropy, charity, and art education, although its main purpose must be thoroughly market-dominant. To be sure, the interplay among art, the art market, and market art is a dynamic process, in which deals are made, lofty art-loving ideals proclaimed, and artworks collected into private hands and into public oblivion, defying a clear line between market art and pure art.

The unfortunate fate of all collectible art is that it cannot exist, much less prosper, without the art market. Every collectible artwork is produced, by its very mode of production, as a *fragmented* work, to be conceived, executed, and collected as a separate entity. While it is inconceivable to collect and own an act or a character in a play, or a measure or an instrumental part in a symphony in any artistically meaningful way, works by collectible artists are inevitably subjected to fragmented existences in separate possessions by collectors through the art market. Even the very idea of a collectible artist surviving and even prospering purely as an artist independent of the market has never been conceived or demonstrated in the ongoing realities of a market society. Ever since art became collectible and marketed when the first royal persona ordered its collection under his private ownership, the two historical phenomena (individual artists and the market), emerging simultaneously in the West, no collectible art or artist has been wholly independent of the market influence.

Today, this market mechanism has progressed—or degenerated, in the opinion of some—to its highest stage of collecting and marketing, ultimately developing into its highest form of commercial sophistication in public persuasion: Namely, art as an elaborate hoax. "The frenzied and much vaunted new explosion of interest in art," observes Robert Wraight, "has nothing to do with art and everything to do with money." In its most progressive form, it is often impossible to tell where art ends and hoax begins. "How long Rothko is going to last?" mused a participant in the famous trial over the Mark Rothko estate in Laurie Adams's account, and his answer shouldn't surprise anyone: "I don't know how long Rothko is going to last. I hope he's going to last long enough for everybody to enjoy the best of the highest prices he can get." Another participant in the case declared that the artist had "outlived the moment of his novelty." This hoax-like quality became so obvious that still another party to the trial said of Rothko's paintings, "There's something wrong when this stuff's palmed off as art." But, he was frank about its basic premise when he said: "We will take the money when we can get it." And as an abstract painter Mark Rothko himself had been unabashedly commercial and was keenly aware of the unpredictable market price. "Today, my price is six thousand or better," he reflected. "Tomorrow it may be six hundred." Even after the thousands of works he had sold while he was alive, the modern abstract painter still left close to 1,000 paintings in his studio when he killed himself.

Although the art market operates like a common enough variation of the marketplace, the commodity it sells in its nature and character, however, is nothing like any other commodity. If the most brilliant con man had to invent a commodity or a trick best suited to hoax, it would easily be art. What sets art apart from other ordinary commodities is essentially its vagueness, arbitrariness, or what I have previously referred to as nothing-ness. When a diamond seller sells his commodity, there is certain stability and predictability expected of the product, price, and quality represented in the transaction. In art commodities there is no such stability or predictability. There is no way of knowing what art is. "Nothing"—in the case of forgeries—as well as "anything"—in the case of the empty canvas—can be sold as art. Such vagueness, arbitrariness, and nothingness that characterize market art is what gives the art market— more specifically, its dealers, its experts, its galleries—the great powers to create and perpetuate the art hoax and, in the process, make or break artists.

As art itself is impossible to define, so is its price. The market price of an artwork is determined in a way unlike any other price mechanism. In highly speculative fields of chance-taking, like the stock market, much non-rational force, sometimes highly sensitive to supernatural and even superstitious elements, is at work in determining a good deal of the decision-making. What appears to be a rational decision is, in such instances, nothing more than a reflection on a dream dreamed the night before, some omen of insignificance, or a wishful reading of tea-leaves. The art pricing is only much more susceptible to such non-rational forces simply because the commodity itself has neither shape, nor character, nor substance, nor stability, nor comparable objectivity. That a canvas with certain colors and figures on it should cost 50 million dollars does indeed require some extraordinary financial foresight or an obsession bordering on insanity to justify the investment.

How then is the art price determined? "By the vibrations set up in the minds of the purchaser," is the answer given by Geraldine Norman in her book on England's best known forger, Tom Keating, who says, "The art market, in fact, is a jungle."

Yet on the surface, at least, the analogy between art market and stock market holds attractive. There are the brokerage houses (art dealers and galleries), the market analysts (art experts and critics), the academic economists (art historians in academia), the investors (art collectors), and the public institutions and organizations dealing in stocks (art museums). But the similarities go no further than this superficial resemblance in organizational form.

For one thing, those who buy and sell in the stock market almost never refer to their doings in honorific, noble, lofty terms. They make no pretenses of serving the public, being dedicated to some lofty philanthropic endeavors, or donating their mighty resources to the preservation of human culture. As vultures and chance-takers of varying stakes, they let everyone know that they are in it for one thing only, namely, money, and nothing more.

But for art-people, since no one really knows why art should be collected and possessed at such enormous prices, it is vital that they embellish their acts with beatific words that befit what they collect and possess. When a wealthy man, essentially uncultured and art-hating, buys an artwork for no other purpose than it is the thing to do with his money, he is hailed as a "devoted art collector" and a "philanthropist" although what he has done is merely taking an artwork into his private possession so that nobody else can enjoy it any more. When an expert gives his opinion—totally arbitrary, not to mention inaccurate—so that an art deal can be made, he is described as a "reputable art expert." Every art dealer, some of the most unsavory businessmen anywhere because of the largely phantom wares they sell to the unsuspecting, possessive fools with money to spend, claims to be an "honest dealer" and a "lover of art," often for generations in the same family, as if simply being a businessman wouldn't be good enough. Strange and bizarre, in a business which is nothing short of a brutal jungle, everyone in the art business feels entitled to great accolades of humanity, nobility, and service.

For another thing, the stock market deals with those stocks whose past performances have demonstrated some predictable and productive qualities. No such predictable or productive qualities ever exist in the art market's wares. The "peculiarities" of the commodities on the art market cannot be overemphasized. Indeed, the public perception that the art market does indeed *have* something it deals, namely, artworks, is the biggest puzzle, if not an outright hoax, yet to be fully understood.

An artwork, whether collectible or uncollectible, is essentially a "surplus" product in society with no practical use. As such, each such product must "manufacture" its own importance or "usefulness" not intrinsic to itself when it claims a market price. Need for a vacuum cleaner doesn't have to be manufactured; need for an artwork does. Indeed, persuading someone to spend huge sums of money to buy a canvas with colors and figures, with no other useful features intrinsic to it, requires some of the most elaborate strategies of mind-manipulation ever known to mankind. Selling art is not unlike persuading a jury: Regardless of the merit or the truth of the case under consideration, both the attorney and the art market must bend the minds of their clients to their cause. The product, as in all other surplus products, must be hyped through the dealer-manipulation of the wealthy but unsure clients. The establishing of "name artists" to entice the vain heart is one of the most common tactics in the art market. It is for this reason for uncertainty associated with surplus existence that the art business (translation: art price) fluctuates wildly and widely according to the general economic indications of society.

The art market's own laws of demand and supply, although superficially in agreement with the general laws of economics, are also of an entirely different kind. Art, especially collectible art, is neither demanded nor supplied by the public which finds no particular usefulness in art (again, not counting the "utilitarian" functions of interior decoration, portrait painting, commercial illustration, personal ornament, etc. among the uses of art). The art market thus finds itself without legitimate demand and supply, which means it must create its own demand—by hype and mind-manipulation about the "value of art" and so on—and its own supply—big name artists, anything-as-art, expanding the collectible artworks into African art, memorabilias of trivial significance, and so on.

As the art market creates and maintains its own demand and supply, it becomes increasingly independent of art and artists, in whose name its demand and supply are created and maintained. Its commodity is capable of self-generating since, especially in modern art, no particular standard of art is required to produce "artworks." Because its commodity is thus independent of artworks in the normal sense, since it can sell anything as art, therefore, the art market ultimately becomes independent of *artists* as well. In this way, the art market requires neither art nor artists to be in business. The art market is fairly self-sustaining, independent of traditional artworks and artists who produce them. If demand is needed, the art market can hype and sell any art form or style to the uncertain and ignorant collector. If supply is needed, the art market can explore any new sources of production as "new art" and a new "star artist," or simply expand its manufacturing capacity. Art and artist have thus become only marginally important to the art market's progress toward its complete independence from them. It is not unlike a company that sells its stocks when it has no public assets.

The final separation of stock market from art market comes in their "openness" and "closeness" as a market respectively. The stock market is an open market, open to the public, its membership depending entirely on the quality of performance by each participant. The art market is a "closed" market: The size of the commodities it deals is limited by the number of the name-artists that it deliberately maintains; the billion dollar business is also held tightly to the chest of its closely-knit members in the art establishment, its membership being limited to a well-guarded elite circle. The limited number of masterworks by name-artists merely change hands, thereby multiplying their price and intensifying the desperate struggle by modern artists to join the market and make it in the big way. The comings and goings of artists in search of a break— the behind-the-scene manipulation in gallery politics—, the big-money corruption of the modern art scene, is indeed worthy of a trashy television mini-saga. (For a glimpse into the art scene, I recommend "The Art of Musical Chairs" in *Vanity Fair*, September 1987, by Anthony Haden-Guest.)

The art market's closedness is an intellectual one as well. As noted, few among members of the general public are able to "decipher" the meaning of this artwork and that, being helplessly dependent on the interpretations provided by experts. This intellectual closedness is inherent in the very nature of collectible art itself—if classic masterworks—as well as in the very progress of its "hoax-ness"—if modern artworks. We shall have occasion to discuss classic and modern art more thoroughly in later chapters.

In the meantime, a series of related questions should be raised: How shall we "open up" the art market? How shall we remove the chains that bind collectible art and the art market into their layers of mystery and hoax? How shall we be able to judge collectible art openly and publicly without the hush-hush that surrounds art and the art market?

To answer the questions, I suggest we return to art forgeries for a new look. As we encountered them earlier in examining the "real-ness" of art, we shall encounter them once again, to unbind collectible art from all its self-protective mystery and hoax. Having examined "real art" from a new point of view and coming to our present conclusion about it, art forgeries now appear slightly different.

Chapter 13

Easy Does It

Let's now compile all known forgeries and the Who's Who of forgery, confining ourselves for convenience to painting only. The names in the parenthesis are the primary source for the information. Their bibliography appears at the end of this book.

Han Van Meegeren forged only eight Vermeers—with a possible ninth hidden somewhere—and two de Hooghs, but the publicity surrounding them made him the grandest forger of them all. (Godley, et al)

Thomas Keating "sexton blaked" English masters like Palmer and Blake as well as the French Impressionists like Degas, Renoir, Sisley; the German Expressionists like Feininger, Nolde, Munch; Goya, Rembrandt, and many others literally in the thousands. (Norman)

According to Norman, there are "dozens" of other professional forgers engaged in forgeries full time, both in England and on the Continent, and the proportion of paintings "whose complete history is known" or can be traced back to the artist himself is "smallish."

Elmyr de Hory, certainly one of the most prolific of forgers, produced at least 2,000 of Picassos, Matisses, Cezannes, Dufys, Modiglianis, Derains, Vlamincks, Renoirs, van Dongens, Bonnards, Chagalls, and others. (Irving)

David Stein, the young forger of modern masters like Chagall, Picasso, Matisse, Cocteau, van Dongen, Dufy, Miro, Derain, and others, one of the fastest producers of fake artworks, made millions of dollars by selling his fakes at his own gallery. (Wraight)

Otto Wacker is known for having painted 30-some Van Goghs, all of which are owned by well known collectors and museums in Europe. (Arnau, Haywood)

Jean Pierre Schecroun, being able to produce a Braque in an hour, ran four salesmen to sell his forgeries all over Europe of Bazaine, Braque, Delaunay, Hartung, Kandinsky, Kupka, Leger, Lhote, Manessier, Miro, Picabia, Picasso, Pollack, Soulages, de Stael, Wols, and others. (Jeppson)

Casper Caspersen's forgeries of fellow Norwegian Edvard Munch are legend for their quality as well as quantity, although there is no evidence that Caspersen forged him "wholesale." (Jeppson)

Lothar Malskat, the legendary creator of the frescoes at the Marienkirche in Lubeck, Germany, had run a "factory" with his partner who pushed the forgeries in canvases and water colors by Barlach, Chagall, Rembrandt, Liebermann, Degas, Corot, Watteau, Utrillo, Munch, Gauguin, Pacin, Rousseau, Hodler, Beckman, Pechstein, and other German Expressionists. (Jeppson)

Millet and Cazot "are credited," according to Jeppson, with "having passed 3,600 counterfeits" in the '55-'65 period.

While stating that "There are, admittedly, hundreds of art forgers," Jeppson, rather incredibly, estimates in his book on art forgeries titled *The Fabulous Frauds* that "at most" art fraud stands at 1 percent of legitimate business, and that 10 percent would be an exaggeration.

A French women's magazine, *Elle*, claimed in 1947 that there were 100,000 fake Utrillos, 1,000 of them properly catalogued as forgeries, in which Maurice Utrillo himself could not tell his real works from fakes, many of which were, after being seized, made into a bonfire by his widow. (Jeppson)

"According to the enlarged edition of his *oeuvre,* Corot painted over 2,000 pictures. Of these, more than 5,000 are in the United States." (quoted in Arnau)

The extent of forgeries is so great that the art establishment stoutly refuses to investigate itself whenever a scandal breaks out because, as Norman observes in connection with the Tom Keating affair, "It would be difficult to know where to stop if such an inquiry were once launched."

(It is interesting to note that Norman and Jeppson are poles apart in their estimates of the extent of forgeries: Norman says in her book on Keating titled *The Fake's Progress* that genuine artworks are a "smallish" proportion; Jeppson, on the other hand, says in the aforementioned book on art forgeries that frauds are no more than one percent while still talking about "hundreds of art forgers whose names and adventures have not been mentioned in this book." What a difference! Norman says *genuine* artworks are "smallish;" Jeppson says *forgeries* amount only to one-to-ten percent. I suppose we should feel vindicated about our earlier estimate of forgeries as roughly one-half as being perfectly reasonable between these two extreme estimates. One thing is clear to us: The precise extent of forgeries is unknown but, based on what is known publicly alone, it is assumed to be fairly large. Without being sarcastic, on the other hand, we can say that, thanks to forgeries, we have *twice as many* artworks in circulation as we otherwise would. (But this last point deserves separate consideration later.)

What causes this persistent and widespread practice of forgery in art? The standard explanation from the art establishment is that the market demands it. While authentic, "real" artworks have become rarer, Jeppson notes, "the number of dealers has increased," with obvious implications for forgeries. "The *market* is the key to art fraud," he also observes. "A shortage of genuine pieces begets imitation." It is Sylvia Hochfield's observation that "unauthorized new castings of works" (a term for forgeries in sculpture) are on the increase because demand "far exceeds supply, and has multiplied dramatically in recent years." Art scholar Peter Fuller agrees by theorizing that art forgery and other forms of corruption materialize only in a society that values property ownership, namely, in Western capitalism. "Historically," he concludes, "forgeries have arisen only where there has been a market in art." Similarly, in the art market, according to Norman, there is tremendous "symbiotic" pressure on art experts and dealers, as well as collectors, to "increase" the volume of artworks with "dubious origins."

This theory of market pressure as an explanation for rampant forgeries goes something like the following:

(1) Experts are often not competent enough to identify real works from forgeries.

(2) Dealers are generally unwilling to apply strict rules of authenticity for reasons of business interest.

(3) Laws of demand and supply in the marketplace are such that forgeries must be produced to fill the gap for masterworks in insufficient supply.

Do these factors explain away the phenomenon of forgery? I think not. Let's switch our mind from the market factor to the factor of the *art medium* itself to help our understanding of the matter. In this new perspective, we find, in response to the above contentions, that:

(1) The art medium is such that experts are unable to identify real artworks from forgeries. In other words, the real-unreal distinction is entirely *impossible* to expertise.

(2) The art medium is such that dealers are unwilling to apply strict rules of authenticity in dealing only with authentic works. In other words, the real-unreal distinction is entirely *unnecessary* in the art business.

(3) The art medium is such that forgeries can meet demand just as well as real artworks do. In other words, the real-unreal distinction is entirely *irrelevant* to art collection.

But what is in the *art medium* as such a powerful force that makes art expertise impossible, the selling of unreal art just as good, and the real-unreal art distinction irrelevant to collectors? My answer, if the reader will forgive me for its simplicity, is that art is THE EASIEST THING TO FORGE AND IMITATE ON THE MARKET. Art is something anybody can *do*. Art forging and imitating is also something anybody can *do* with a modicum of talent in copying someone's pictures. In classics, one needs good mastery of techniques; in modern art, one doesn't even need that. In spite of all the mystery associated with art, or perhaps because of it, art is a fairly easy thing to copy, fake, forge, imitate, and duplicate. Hence the extent of forgeries. It is not unlike trying to be the guru of some obscure religious sect or a television evangelist: All one needs is the ability to convince people that he is genuine. Perhaps it is for this reason that guru-ship and televangelism have always attracted some of the most unsavory phonies and con men who strive for easy success.

After giving this simple secret out as to why there are so many forgeries in the midst of real stuff, I am going to state what amounts to the "Law of Forgery" thusly: FORGERY INCREASES IN CORRECT PROPORTION TO THE EASE OF FORGED OBJECTS AND TO THE SIZE OF REWARDS TO GAIN. This law reiterates what has been obvious to the reader. Forgeries of Object X exist where (1) it is *easy* to forge Object X; and (2) the forger can bring in a *lot of money* from the forgeries of Object X. Just imagine, going back to the art market, how "easy" it is to fool experts with forgeries, and how "expensive" these forged works are. The collector, in his infinite ignorance and possessiveness, is willing to pay any amount for a name-painting; the dealer, in his usual businessman's desire for profit, is willing to sell anything that can pass for art, as anything usually does; and the expert, in his position between collector and dealer, loses nothing and gains everything by authenticating the forged work. This way, everyone is happy.

All these factors combined, it would certainly be foolish for any struggling but talented artist *not* to try forgeries for easy money. It amounts to a minor miracle that we do not have *more* forgeries. Of all things that can be faked and profitable so easily, collectible art stands above everything. Compare art forgery with two things: One, forgery in its sister art forms, namely, uncollectibles. Two, forgery in common goods and services.

First, forgery in uncollectible art. It is generally impossible to forge an artwork attributable to a famous uncollectible artist. There has never been a successful forgery that fooled everyone in the musical, literary or dramatic world. (We shall return to this subject once again later.)

Second, forgery in common goods and services. We often hear that famous brand-names in jeans, watches, handbags, and so on, are faked by cheaper imitators. While this sort of faking obviously goes on, notice that the faked goods and services must have some *material reality* for what they are substituting. One cannot just substitute something real (a real watch) with something unreal (no watch). The quality of the latter may not be *as good* as the former, but, nevertheless, some resemblance of parity in material quality must be there. A fake Swiss watch has to *run* like a watch; a pair of fake jeans must wear like jeans, at least for a while; a fake handbag must look, feel, and work like a handbag.

In the world of forgery, art forgery commands a superior position simply because of its ease in forging it. Many well known forgers have confessed that Picasso is the easiest painter to forge, imitate, or copy. Why? Because Picasso's artworks are rather very simple, so simple and numerous—owing to the simplicity—in fact that Picasso himself was unable to tell his own works from possible fakes in his name. Even among those artists who have been forged by others, the most prohibitively difficult artists—say, Michelangelos, Leonardos, Raphaels—have been less frequently attempted than many of the modern and contemporary artists whose works are technically easier to forge. In the latter group, abstract artworks, we are told, are the easiest marks for forgers, due to their simplicity in conception and ease of execution. In some cases of Conceptual Art, Minimalism, or whatever—as in Jo Baer's "empty canvas' —virtually *anybody* could copy their artworks. Hence the Law of Forgery.

That forging in collectible art is explained chiefly by its ease can be further elaborated in the following:

(1) It is easy to *complete* a collectible artwork. Aside from the huge frescoes like Michelangelo's in the Sistine Chapel, most collectible artworks take a relatively short time to complete, from a few minutes to a few days. Elmyr de Hory, as a justification for his forgeries, once described Picasso's production of artworks as done "between the two puffs of his cigar." Virtually every artwork in collectible art is executed in fragments, as a piece that is small and can be easily framed and stored. While varying in the plan, size, and effort of each work executed, nevertheless, most collectible art comes in dosages of small, manageable proportions. Some have small plans; some minuscule sizes; some requiring only a minimum effort, to complete the work. It is nothing like completing a play, a symphony, a novel, or a philosophical treatise. For this reason of easy completion, collectible artists tend to be prolific with their opuses, producing thousands upon thousands of artworks almost like a factory machine. In fact some artists and forgers could produce artworks faster than a machine. It would be asking too much of posterity to treat each of their works as a precious artwork of enormous significance.

As it is easy to complete, it is also easy to "comprehend," perhaps in a few seconds of looking at it. Even with some of the "great" works, we spend less than a few moments in looking at them. Experts can say anything they wish about the "meaning" of this artwork and that, and this artist and that, or about how long it takes to get to know all the profound meanings of this art or that artist. But there is no point in arguing with experts or anyone else over this issue. For, if one can get a profound "meaning" out of a nothing, like the empty canvas and the shovel, or an elegant lady of the Renaissance, I am sure one can get all sorts of meaning out of just about anything. But, after all, viewing a painting or a sculpture is nothing like reading a serious novel, listening to a symphony, or mulling over a deep philosophy.

(2) It is easy to *become* an artist of collectible art. The range between great artists and most incompetent artists is indeed great, but they all go by the title of *artist*. There are millions of "artists" in the United States alone and their levels of competence as artists must surely vary as much as their number. The "technique" of being an artist varies also. Depending on what kind of artist one wants to be, one's technical mastery need not be very great indeed. Many retired people take up painting as a hobby; housewives dabble in drawing between house chores; "art therapists" teach their mentally-incompetent charges to paint pictures for therapy. How much technical competence is indeed required for the essentially honorific title of artist? Especially in "modern art," it appears that sometimes no skill whatsoever is needed to call oneself an artist. This paucity of technical mastery is true, it seems, even in some of the most vaunted and expensive artworks. But more than anything else,

(3) It is easy to be *original* with one's artwork in collectible art. The very fact that collectible art is so easily faked and forged proves the *commonness* of the concept embodied in the original artwork. Every canvas is considered an original artwork as long as the artist signed it. Unless they are machine-produced, all artworks are treated as "originals." But, this way, the meaning of originality is made completely meaningless in collectible art. Why should it be so difficult to copy the style of a La Tour, Van Gogh, Picasso, or Pollock, to the extent that there is no difference between the two? There is then, corollary to the Law of Forgery above, the truism that A TRULY ORIGINAL WORK OF ART CANNOT BE FORGED, perhaps imitated as the best form of flattery but not duplicated. It would be absolutely unthinkable for someone to fake a Beethoven symphony in his characteristic style of vigor and dynamics, because we *know* that it is Beethoven's style and no one is original enough to come up with another piece that would pass for a Beethoven. Most of Beethoven's 100-some works are so different from one another that rarely is one work a close copy of another in style, theme, or character. Picasso is credited to have "invented" cubism, but how many times did he himself paint cubist pictures *over and over* for the rest of his life? It would be unthinkable for Beethoven to have composed 30 variations—not to mention 3,000—on the famous "Fifth Symphony" theme and called them all "originals."

Originality in collectible art is easy to achieve largely because each changing *subject* matter is credited with originality. When Van Gogh paints sunflowers we say it is an original painting. Then he shifts his subject to irises and paints them exactly *in the same style*, we say it is an original painting. But how could they both be two *originals*? Both are exactly the same in style, just two variations on the same theme. If one has seen one, one has seen them all. Similarly, most artists both classic and modern have painted the same pictures over and over all their lives, and they are sold as separate originals!

(It is not unlike the detective mysteries of Agatha Christie or the symphonies of Franz Joseph Haydn, whose works would be easy marks for talented forgers only if there were enough money in their forgeries. It was sometimes said that Haydn wrote the same symphony a hundred and four times over, and a movement from one symphony could be easily substituted for one in another. Something similar might be said about Christie's murder stories, for her settings and characters were so repetitiously similar that they could easily be interchangeable with one another. That Haydn's symphonies were all beautiful or that Christie's mysteries were all entertaining is an altogether different matter. It is just that their works are relatively easy to forge for their essential lack of originality.)

In view of what collectible artists paint, all their variations are imitations of their *own* originals, for which there is usually one original created by each artist unless they undergo radical stylistic changes in their career. Thus true originality must consist not only of one artist being different from *another* artist, but also of his works being different from *his own* other works. It would be impossible to call *all* of Picassos or Van Goghs original works of art, simply because they are the many variations of the same theme with practically no stylistic changes in them. They merely changed the subject for each painting, which can hardly be said to be original. One artwork after another, Picasso produced the endlessly same Picassos; so did Van Gogh to a lesser extent; so did Rembrandt; so did Pollock; so did...Why couldn't or wouldn't someone else do another Picasso, another Van Gogh, another Rembrandt, another Pollock, and so on, a relatively easy task for a huge sum of money as long as their imitative quality could pass?

Perhaps it is in the nature of collectible art that the artist *cannot* be original with his art often enough to vary his style, theme, or character to be original with every artwork he produces. Perhaps it is just too much to expect. But then we shouldn't be surprised to know that their repetitious works cannot be protected from forgers and fakers. The very nature of painting (or sculpture) is such that no artist's style can remain protected as original from later forgers and fakers. And many of their stylistic differences are not terribly original from one another's. If each artist created all his works in *different* styles, they could never be forged. Since there would be only one work of that distinction, another one like it would be instantly known to be a forgery. In his prolific productivity and with his peculiar art medium, however, no artist can be *this* original with his art.

One may say whatever one wishes about Picasso as an artist, but I don't happen to believe that his cubist style is so prohibitively original in the annals of all art, both collectible and uncollectible, as to be the symbol of his exclusive artistic monument. I once attended an art lecture given by a Mr. Warren Robbins from the Smithsonian on the connection between African art and modernism, who convincingly demonstrated that Picasso's style was a wholesale adoption of many native African artifacts. Whatever his contributions to art history, originality couldn't be one. Technically and conceptually, many modern collectible artworks often approach children's play, which makes the claim of exclusive originality with each work all the more difficult to sustain and honor.

Art forgery, as we have seen, is instrumental for us in two ways: It contributes to the art market, in meeting demand by increasing supply. More importantly, perhaps, it helps us expose and unmask the arbitrariness, the emptiness, the superficialness—in short, the "hoax"—of the art establishment.

We shall continue with the latter task.

Chapter 14

Would the Real Art Stand Up?

On May 1, 1978 a much-anticipated exhibition of nine Pollocks opened at the Ivan Dougherty Gallery sponsored by the Art School of Alexander Mackie College of Advanced Education, Sydney, Australia. However, two strange things happened with the exhibition.

First, questions were raised about the authenticity of the Pollocks because some people thought they might be forgeries. A Mr. Reinhard, the Dean of the School of Art at the College, who organized the exhibition, was of the opinion that "It would be as difficult to prove the 'Pollocks' were fake as to prove that they were genuine." With this simple statement, reflecting the general sentiment of the art establishment, he demonstrated that, with rare exceptions of material discrepancy, there is really no *difference* between real art and fake art.

Second, five of the nine "Pollocks" were thought by some as being hung *"upside down"*. When asked about this confusing hanging of the pictures, Mr. Reinhard said, "Five of the nine are either shown upside down in the catalogue or have been mounted upside-down in the frames. We hung them according to the way they are framed and left it at that." This episode, which seems to be a minor one in the hectic world of art exhibitions, points to another incongruence about art, especially modern art, that there is really no *difference* between a picture hung right side up or a picture hung upside down. In fact it would have mattered little or nothing if the Pollocks were hung on their *sides*, no one would have noticed them and no one would have cared.

Suppose, just so that the point is made clear, the exhibitors went to Pollock's studio to pick up his paintings. They found a picture laying on the floor with some figures on it which was actually a canvas on which one of his guests accidentally spilt some colors. Not knowing that this was the origin of the new "Pollock" the exhibitors hung it along with other legitimate ones at the gallery, and just accidentally on *its side*. Would anyone *know* the difference and *care* about the origin or the position of the "painting"?

There are other similar episodes that are equally baffling and contradictory to our commonsense and logic.

When two versions of Sir Peter Paul Rubens's "Diana and Her Nymphs" were sold to Paul Getty and the Cleveland Museum of Art respectively, controversies arose as to which one was the real one. Experts lined up on both sides, claiming one was the real one and the other a forgery. Overserving this tussle the *Sunday Express* commented that "The painting which is finally acclaimed as the original deserves to rank in importance besides Rubens's 'Adoration of the Magi.' " Notice that both were purchased by prestigious sources at great prices, that the pictures were "good" enough to be claimed by experts as genuine Rubens, and that, according to the strange observation of the press above, one picture would have to be declared to rank with the best, and the other to "be comparatively worthless." But the question, and the irony, is which one will be the real one destined to rank with the best, and which one the forgery to be thrown in the trash can? It is not unlike two Miss Universes, each claiming the crown and supported by one half of the judges; but in this case, there would be one Miss Universe and one *runner up*. This reasonable conclusion, of courses, does not apply in the case of the two Rubenses. The task is made no easier by the fact that, according to Wraight, "When so much money is at stake...owners of paintings are often understandably reluctant to get at the truth." We can see why owners would be reluctant to know the truth, but the real truth for us is that either way it doesn't matter. Wraight calls it "crazy illogic of the art game, a house of cards built on the, often infirm, shoulders of the experts."

The "Vermeers" which Han Van Meegeren painted, when properly certified as real Vermeers by authorities, were valued at what would be close to 50 million dollars in today's price. After Van Meegeren had confessed to his forgery, however, the market value of the same paintings dropped instantly to zero. (The figures have been calculated from John Godley's 1940s estimate.) Why? What does that mean? One can say, superficially, about the fluctuations of art prices; one can say about the inflated values of artworks. But neither explains anything about the violent changes in their value. The truth is that neither love for art nor art price has *anything* to do with art, for the same artworks could not be "loved" and "valued" in one instance and dropped in the next for no reason, or for any reason, entirely *unrelated* to the artworks in question.

Consider, also, the case of Texas oil millionaire and collector Algur Meadows again, who had built up a large collection of Impressionist and post-Impressionist paintings. As Peter Fuller describes it, "Meadows was proud of the works, and spoke of his enjoyment of them." However, when the forgers (Elmyr de Hory and his ring) had been caught and the collection proven mostly fakes, the same Meadows "then wanted to get rid of these very same paintings at once." Either Meadows's love for art was extremely shallow and superficial, or the paintings he had dearly loved had turned bad overnight.

When the 30-some Van Goghs appeared in Otto Wacker's gallery in Berlin a trial was held, upon complaints by some dealers that they were forgeries. Different experts gave different testimonies, some of which we have seen earlier. Expert opinions were divided into the following four groups according to what they saw in the Van Goghs, as told by Arnau:

Group One: All the pictures are real Van Goghs.

Group Two: Some are real Van Goghs and some fakes.

Group Three: All the pictures are fakes.

Group Four: Some are real Van Goghs and some fakes, but this group's real and fake Van Goghs are not the same as Group Two's real and fake Van Goghs.

Similar to the Rubens case in illogic and absurdity, the Van Gogh case seems slightly more complicated, however. Otto Wacker received one year's prison sentence for fraud, but the question of which Van Goghs were real and which ones not was never resolved. All of them are still owned by prestigious collectors and institutions.

Alceo Dossena, the maker of sculpture in any style and of any age, was the subject of superlatives and adulation in the twenties when he was *not* known as himself but as the well known masters for whose works his own passed. When, after fifty years or so of complete anonymity, he suddenly became internationally famous for his numerous forgeries, experts, some of whom had given his works the greatest accolades, now red-faced, became mercilessly critical about the artistic worth of his works. For us, the puzzle is obvious, Why is Dossena a great artist when he is someone else well known, and a mere worthless forger when he is being himself? Frank Arnau considers Dossena a rare link between "actuality" (real art) and "appearance" (fake art). But is actuality really actual, and appearance really without substance? How can unreality pass for reality so long, certified virtually by every known authority who, after the confession of forgery, instantly turns against the real art that he himself had certified? Was "actuality" really actual to begin with, if it can be so easily replaced by un-actuality and the replacement so praised and revered by everyone?

The controversial La Tour called "The Fortune Teller," which still hangs in the Metropolitan Museum of Art, stood in the 60s "in official terms as a *masterpiece*," in spite of the fact that it was "denounced" by a prominent art expert. By the 70s its "credentials firmly established," it was "accepted by every other La Tour authority" as genuine. But it was obviously a forgery, according to the subsequent investigations made on it by Christopher Wright who wrote a whole book detailing the "wrongness" of "The Fortune Teller." What happens now to the picture's "credentials" as a "masterpiece" certified by "every other La Tour authority"?

Told in Flemming's book on forgery detection, there was an unfinished female figure sculpted in marble which had been thought to be the work of Michelangelo, which was accordingly considered worth a fortune. A scientific investigation revealed that the sculpture had been worked on through a "pointing process," apparently a "mechanical method" known to have been shunned by the Renaissance master. This fact made it now instantly worthless. But the account does not satisfy us as to why a work good enough to be a Michelangelo is now no longer good enough only because they discovered what tool was used on the artwork.

Finally, we can remind ourselves of the artists, especially those prolific ones, who could not tell their own works from forged ones. Elmyr de Hory's account of Picasso and Kees van Dongen who failed the test, and the court testimony of Utrillo who said he was unable to distinguish his own works from fakes—whose widow threw many of the forgeries into a bonfire while *doubting* they were really fake Utrillos—are classics. Then there is the episode of Laurence Stephen Lowry, told by Wraight, who was shown a fake purportedly by him and told the purchaser that he had bought a bogus Lowry. Upon being told so, the purchaser did not believe Lowry's authority on his *own* paintings. "Are you sure it isn't yours?" the purchaser asked in doubt. "Isn't there some expert I could take it to for an opinion?" (The Lowry episode is told in Wraight)

These stories, although told as amusing anecdotes in the art circle and receiving only cursory attention from writers, tell us as much about art itself as they do about art forgery. But most writers on forgery *assume* and *defend* that art is real and forgery unreal. They never ask what *allows* such a proliferation of forgeries in art, or what is wrong *with art* that, more often than not, cannot be distinguished from non-art. The contradictions, illogic, and absurdities that abound in the above stories— and in many other such anecdotes that make the rounds in the art establishment—must somehow be resolved to our satisfaction. What the writers generally try to avoid is in itself a contradiction: They tell all the stories of art contradictions, illogic, and absurdities *without* hurting the very art business itself. What they are saying is basically this: Look, art is the most contradictory, illogical, and absurd thing there is, and we have plenty of stories to tell you proving that it is so. But we insist that art is still legitimate and forgery illegitimate, art good and forgery bad, and art beautiful and forgery ugly. Never mind that every story we tell you contradicts that very assumption about art.

The whole concept of "real art" hinges on its authenticity, that is, the signature on the canvas or the sculpture, or whatever. But consider the two alternative explanations in *every case* under consideration: The real-forgery controversy cannot be possible unless (1) the work is so *good* that it is thought *as good* as the ones that are regarded as authentic works by the purported artist; or (2) the *signature* of the *original artist* is so good that it can be put on *any* work and make the work a good work of art by the powers of the signature alone.

Now, consider the mind-boggling dilemma this real-unreal controversy brings out in *every* case:

If (1) is true, then the question of whether or not Artwork X is by the purported artist—the whole notion of authenticity in art itself—is wholly *irrelevant*. In this case we are only interested in whether Artwork X is "good enough," not whether it is indeed by Artist Y. So "name"—whether a Michelangelo, a Van Gogh, a Picasso, or a "nobody" — becomes of no particular significance. Every artwork must prove its own quality as art, and nothing else matters.

If (2) is true, then *art* itself becomes *impossible* because it is the *signature*, not the artistic worth of Artwork X, that matters. If anything can be turned into art as long as it has a recognizable "name" regardless of how "good" the work is, then we can no longer talk about art as something real and achievable and artistic as something judged as valuable and admirable. We can only talk about signatures. What we would find real, achievable, valuable, and admirable would be the *signature*, not Artwork X itself. So no longer can art exist if this is true.

This dilemma can be restated this way:

If (1) is true, then *art business* is impossible. It won't be able to sell a Michelangelo for millions and an unknown for a dollar purely on the basis of their name-recognition. Every artwork would have to be judged by its own merit and the art-forgery distinction, the life blood of art business, would become impossible to sustain. Its business is made possible only by being able to say about work X, yes, it is art, and about Y, no it is not art. If it cannot do this, there is no art business.

If (2) is true, then *art* itself is impossible as an endeavor, for the name-signature would be everything and art itself nothing. No matter how good Artwork X, if its signature is not a name-signature, it won't matter and it is a rather demoralizing thought. All so-called artworks would be judged solely by their signatures, not how good they are.

The standard attempt to resolve this dilemma—the expert-incompetence factor—has already been considered and discarded. The only factor that we must consider, finding no other way out of it, is indeed that ART ITSELF IS INCAPABLE OF LEGITIMATE EXISTENCE OR LOGICAL EXPLANATION.

If there were no money involved in the real-forgery controversies and flip-flop histories, we would simply consider such illogic to be the very nature of art and leave it at that. Thus, art may be proven illogical and there is much evidence to support this view, but *art business* cannot. For art business, unlike art, is a coldly calculating, rationally conceived, and efficiently operating business enterprise that has nothing to do with the illogic and mystic nature of art and artists. Art may be all that is unclear, and the artist slightly irrational, but art business is none of this. It is simple selling and buying. But what it sells and buys is so thoroughly mixed up with what is called art and its enormous price fluctuations that it complicates the issue.

Art business, in essence, is the only business which sells *nothing* for *something* at an enormous price of its own creation. Not unlike the gold vs. brass comparison between real art and forgery suggested by Waldron earlier, Wraight compares real butter (real art) with margarine (forgery) as a case in which the latter passes for the former. Is it fair? he asks. Of course, on the face of it, it isn't fair. But upon reflection, we see something else: What if (1) margarine is as good as real butter, (2) no expert in the world can tell or experts are divided over its genuineness, (3) there is no harm in taking the latter as former, (4) admittedly there has been a butter-margarine mixture of 50-50 being used all over the world, and (5) some packages, with a label as butter, costs millions and some packages, branded as margarine, are discarded as fakery? What does it say about the real butter and the market that concocts such a trickery? we might ask.

We can see that the art-forgery controversy exists only if there is a huge price on artworks, and if artworks can be collected and possessed by individual owners. But whether it is the *price* or it is the *possession* that triggers the controversy, *neither* is relevant to art.

First, about price. That artworks are sold for a price has nothing to do with art, for art thrives just as well whether there is money in it or not. All that every artist wants, assuming his intentions are truly artistic and not mercenary, is his freedom to paint. Ninety-nine percent of artists in the world at any time barely scratch out a living from selling their artworks at any rate, and great fortunes would be the last thing they have in mind when they think about art.

Second, about possession. That artworks are collected and possessed by prominent individuals is a fact that is neither universal as a cultural practice—for it is not so in the Orient and non-market cultures—, nor ubiquitous as a historical fact—for it is true only with the emergence of individual property ownership. Artworks are artworks whether they are displayed on streetcorners, exhibited in great museums of art, or owned exclusively by wealthy private owners. Neither art nor the artist could care less about the disposition of artworks.

In both cases, of course, we could not assume otherwise either about art or about artists.

The simple fact so easily overlooked in art-forgery controversies is that there is so *much* or so *little* in art—depending on one's opinion on art—that an artwork can be the greatest masterpiece if everything (signature, expert testimony, publicity) falls into place, or worthless junk if something goes wrong with the same work (suspected of fakery, gossip about authenticity, bad publicity). Now, mind you, in either case, whether a masterpiece or worthless junk, we are talking about the *same* artwork which *can be both*. How can something be a masterpiece *and* junk, we might ask, unless the very criteria for masterpiece-junk are thoroughly irrelevant to begin with? A work is hailed as a masterpiece; that same day it falls to disgrace when found to be a forgery; the next day it is hailed as a masterpiece once again because they realize that they had made a mistake; the next day they call it junk because they found once again reason to suspect it was a forgery; then the next day... Obviously this scenario is not plausible in reality—although the Met's 5th century B.C. Greek bronze horse comes close to this flip-flop—, but its theoretical implication is not too far removed from our actual experience.

Let's take a familiar example to drive our point home once again.

The often quoted reference to the necessity of revolution in society to overthrow an unjust government, attributed to both Thomas Jefferson and V.I. Lenin, is a case in point. College students flip-flop over the statement. They tend to agree with the statement if they *think* it is made by Jefferson, and, conversely, disagree with the same statement if it is identified as Lenin's view of revolution. The conclusion we can draw from this real life contradiction, in relation to the flip-flop in art above, is this: The statement itself is so ambiguous and imprecise that two thinkers from two opposite poles—capitalism and Communism—can say the same thing without contradiction. Students change their opinions on the issue with such irregularity precisely because the issue which they are asked to judge is so unclear. Suppose it can be proven that Jefferson actually said wealth should be owned by all workers and peasants, but not by a few wealthy individuals—which is a basic Communist idea—, and American students are asked to react to it. They will then have to choose between (1) agreeing that, since they admire Jefferson no matter what he says, it is a good idea and all become Communists; and (2) disagreeing with Jefferson, because they cannot agree with a Communist idea, they now revise their opinion of Jefferson as a Communist. Strangely enough, this sort of logical change of heart never occurs in the art world regarding forgery.

There are many artworks exhibited in great museums that are considered "possible" forgeries. Upon reflection, this is a strange, question-begging description of an artwork. What does it mean that it is a "possible" forgery? Does that mean it is "possibly art" and "possibly no-art" ? How could something be possibly art and possibly no-art at the same time? Is there anything, even a forgery, that has absolutely no "artistic value"? Of course, this contradiction can be resolved easily if we consider that the criteria for possible art-no art are just sheer nonsense in the first place, whereby the very notion of art itself is sheer nonsense. No other such yes-no criteria in our true life—real doctor-fake doctor, real pilot-fake pilot, real diamond-fake diamond, for familiar examples— could tolerate the contradictions, illogic, and absurdities of the art world. What is amazing is that such ambiguities of art are regularly mixed with precise money figures which, miraculously, do not experience such ambiguities. Of course, art prices are *prices* for commodities, they have nothing to do with art although they are paid *to art* in each instance.

What are we to make of all such nonsense?

Chapter 15

If Nothing is Something, Then...

There are basically two positions held among writers regarding the art-forgery issue: The majority and minority positions.

The majority position, as in all other cases, represents the obvious "party line" or orthodox view of the art establishment: That, forgery *is* forgery and art *is* art, and the two are as diametrically opposed to each other as night and day, life and death, truth and falsity, and the two shall never meet. At least in theory, the position holds that there is no doubt that art and forgery have nothing in common and shall never be thought of as belonging in the same category. Law enforcement stands behind this position; expertise is enlisted to detect forgery; and the public is encouraged to condemn forgery as the scourge of all that is honorable, respectable, and beautiful. Most books written on forgeries, with the exceptions noted below, support this view of art and forgery.

The minority position, a view supported by some writers and philosophers for different reasons—and by a fairly large segment of the public especially at a time when a forger emerges as a folk hero after a scandal as in the cases involving Van Meegeren, Keating, Dossena, and others—asserts that forgery is or should be regarded as *art*, every bit as honorable, respectable, and beautiful as "real art." Tom Keating's supporter Geraldine Norman and Van Meegeren's sympathizer-biographer John Godley, along with a smattering of philosophers for a different reason, have actively voiced this opinion in support of forgeries as part of the mainstream art establishment. Their position is somewhat akin to socialists in a capitalist society, a segment in sympathy with forgers as underdogs against the powerful Establishment.

Both positions, however, are in agreement as regards the distinction between art and forgery. The former argues that the distinction should remain, art as everything and forgery as nothing. The latter argues that, while the distinction is valid, forgery is not as insignificant as the former argues, and should be treated with more respect.

These two positions as standard responses separating the issue confound us immediately. For neither seems satisfactory. Why?

If the first view (forgery-as-forgery, art-as-art) is held true, as we have seen, how do we explain the fact that up to one-half of all collectible art—and perhaps much more in certain collectibles, such as African art—is forgery? The problem with this position is simply *what to do with forgery*, both as a concept and as a reality. It is all very well to insist on the distinction between real art and forgery. But this is not only *impossible* in view of the difficulty in telling the two apart, but it is also *undesirable* in view of the necessity to create forgeries in order to meet the increasing demand for famous artworks as their supply is either limited or dwindling. The position is a conventional and safe one to hold. But its implication in reality is nothing short of blatant hypocrisy and insurmountable contradiction.

If the second view (forgery-as-art) is held true, on the other hand, the situation does not improve much. If these writers, philosophers, and some disgruntled members of the public insist that forgery *is* art and should be treated so, how do they propose to explain their view that non-art (that is, forgery) *is* or *can be* art? Art and forgeries are two distinctive categories that cannot be blended into one without doing violence to commonsense and logic. It's like saying all opposites are really the same thing, and night is no different from day, black from white, real from unreal, and so on. There are two distinct reasons among supporters to hold this position. Writers like Norman and Godley say that, since the art establishment itself is corrupt, keeping forgeries out of art circulation as non-art—especially in the case of Keating and Van Meegeren—is highly hypocritical. Some philosophers have argued that there may be some historical documentary functions in forgeries. But neither opinion insists that forgery *is* indeed art. They are saying, yes, forgery is forgery, no doubt about it, but it should be treated *like* real art. But this position still leaves the issue unresolved, and still basically at the mercy of the art establishment, which considers the argument and rejects it.

Readers who have been following my arguments seriously so far can now anticipate a *third* position: That, in view of the illogic and contradiction of the above two positions, the conclusion to draw from the issue is that, yes, FORGERY IS NO ART, BUT NEITHER IS ART ITSELF. IF FORGERY IS A DECEPTION, SO IS ART ITSELF. IF FORGERY IS A HOAX, SO IS ART ITSELF.

There are no other ways out of the dilemma. The first view we considered above cannot explain away *forgery*. The second view cannot explain away *art*. The first is contradicted by forgery, the second by art. We can insist upon the first only if forgery is nonexistent in its midst or easily separable from the real stuff, or its intrusion is minimal. We can insist upon the second, on the other hand, only if we can nullify the very idea of art, rather than wanting to strengthen it by insisting upon joining it with forgery.

Either way, they still leave the art-forgery issue intact. Our third approach is that, while art uncovers the non-artness of forgery, forgery actually helps us uncover the non-artness of art. Hence the inevitable conclusion that art is forgery, or put in another way, art is non-art. Let's clarify this further and pull our thoughts together by considering the following observations.

One, consider the "emotional responses" that forgeries—of Van Meegeren, Keating, Dossena, and others—evoke in experts as well as the general public. The original emotional reactions are real, not phony or staged, since they have no idea that they are looking at forgeries. They are exactly the same kind of emotional reactions that are evoked when looking at genuine artworks. But, how can the real thing be "real" when a fake can get the same reaction from the viewer? Compare it with diamonds. If a fake diamond can do all the things that a real diamond can, how can we say the real diamond is really "real" when we have to admit that fakes (no diamond) are the same as the real ones?

Two, consider a variation from the above, in which (1) *no response* is evoked from *real* art, and (2) a *real response* is evoked from *no art*. There are many instances, confirmed easily by our personal experience, in which we get *nothing* out of particular artworks while viewing them. Sometimes we are incapable of producing our own response, sometimes the artworks we are viewing fail to evoke any emotion from us. On the other hand, some people—especially art experts—have their emotional responses evoked by "nothings," such as the "empty canvas" noted before or other nonsense works that make absolutely no sense to other people. How is "nothing" (no response) evoked from "something" (real art)? On the other hand, how is "something" (real response) evoked from "nothing" (an empty canvas as art, for example)? Unless we conclude that the response is phony or staged, which it is not, the only conclusion is that there is *no difference* between "something" (real art) and "nothing" (anything-as-art). Is there any other possibility from this?

Three, related to the two observations above, consider this: If the viewer's response can be evoked either from a "real" artwork, or from a "nothing" posing as an artwork, or from a "non-real" artwork (forgery) equally easily, then whatever the viewer is looking at makes absolutely no difference. It cannot be the source of the viewer's emotion. The viewer's emotional response, in this case, is determined by the viewer *himself*, not the *object* he is looking at, because whether he is looking at real art, or nothing-as-art, or non-real art, the response is entirely *his*, not the object's. His response has nothing to do with the art (or non-art) object. *Any* object, whether art or non-art, would then be able to evoke the emotional response from the viewer. *Any* object, by the same token, no matter what it is, can also *fail* to evoke such emotion. What, if both are true which they are, is this thing called art when no-art can do the same thing?

Four, consider the case in which Artwork X is argued to be *both* real and unreal in all authenticity controversies. If an artwork can be equally real *and* unreal, how can we say that "realness" and "unrealness" really matter? For Artwork X to be *either* art *or* forgery, it has to be able to be categorized as such, one or the other, for the artwork cannot be *both* art *and* forgery. When it cannot be settled by any known human means, if we recall all the experts who died believing in their own opinions as sincerely as those who held opposite opinions, therefore, the only conclusion possible is that the categories of real art and non-real art are wholly invalid. Hence, art is non-art and non-art is art, which makes no sense at all.

Five, recalling our discussion in an earlier chapter, consider the case in which if nothing can be something easily and without distinction, then the something *must be* nothing. If over one-half of all "something" (real art) can be substituted by "nothing" (forgery), with expert testimony and with no harmful effects from the mix-up, then the "something" must be really "nothing." To conform to our commonsense and logic, we can see that the substitution can take only one of the following categories: (1) Nothing happens *only if* nothing substitutes nothing, which are identical with each other (substitute water with water, air with air, or nothing with nothing). (2) Something *must happen* if nothing substitutes for something, which are radically incompatible with each other (substitute sand for gasoline, air for water, or nothing for something). If nothing (non-art or forgery) can substitute something (real art) easily, massively, and with no difference, how can we say that the something is really something?

Six, recalling that identifying art authenticity is difficult, gathering obviously from the difficulties that experts, for all their expertise, experience everyday and widely, we have no other way of explaining it except that there is *nothing* to identify in art. If what they are to identify is artistic, in the sense of how "beautiful" or "aesthetic" the work is, then *who* painted it is irrelevant. If what they are to identify is technical, in the sense of whose *signature* it is on the canvas, then *artistic* consideration (how "good") is irrelevant. If we conclude from this that *anything* is and can be art, because neither the how-good nor the whose-signature is relevant, then just as inevitably we must conclude that art is *nothing*. How else are we to think? If the art establishment says they are really trying to see *how good* Artwork X is, then how do they explain the fact that they sell anything that bears the "right" name or signature? If the art establishment says, on the other hand, they are really trying to see if the *signature* is correct as a way of determining good art, how do they explain the fact that they discard or condemn good art only because the signature is "wrong"?

Seven, reconsider this dilemma one more time: How can something be something one day—when Artwork X is believed to be real—then be nothing the next—when it is discovered to be a forgery, as Texan collector Meadows has demonstrated—then be something again the very next day when the discovery is "discovered" to have been wrong, as happened with the 5th century, B.C. Greek bronze horse at the Metropolitan Museum of Art in New York—unless, whatever it is, the "something" is really "nothing" to begin with. Look at it yet in another way through our more familiar daily experience. Bob confesses his love for Jane but the very next day his armourous feeling abruptly cools when he discovered that Jane's name was actually Susan, a small mistake with her birth-certificate that she had just discovered herself. Susan pleads with him that she is, after all, the *same* person he had found lovable only yesterday, and that the Jane-Susan issue is really a minor, insignificant, merely technical one that, if he truly loved her, should not matter at all. But Bob, in the real-life fashion of Algur Meadows with his newly-discovered forgeries, is anxious "to get rid of" Jane-Susan. What can we say about the "realness" or "substance" of his confessed love for Jane? Is there anything else to say other than that it was nonexistent or it was something other than love (in Meadows's case instant culture, in Bob's case perhaps her name, both of which have nothing to do with art and love respectively). We have no other way of saying than that Meadows's love for art and Bob's love for Jane were both phony, phantom, and nonexistent, in short—since they deliberately posed it as real for a while—an elaborate hoax.

Every controversy over forgeries, as we can see now, only proves the nothingness—literally and metaphorically—of collectible art and the emptiness of the claim to the contrary by the art establishment. Thus, every forgery that emerges controversial contributes to the unmasking of phony, phantom, and nonexistent art.

One of the ways in which the claim for the "realness" of art—almost exclusively in collectible art, that is—is carried out has been the increasing inroad that "scientific detection" has made into the business of art authenticity. More and more, technology and machines are making the final pronouncement on whether Artwork X is real or not, replacing the traditional connoisseurs from their accustomed trade. In the last two decades or so, this technical replacement of aesthetics has been especially prominent. Removing the credibility of "intuition," observes Christopher Wright, one of the old-line experts who "proved" the La Tour "Fortune Teller" to be a forgery, "Some scientists have become all-powerful and now make pronouncements on the attribution of pictures." In other words, what used to be judged chiefly by visual inspection and secondarily by scientific means is now being judged chiefly by machines and secondarily by the human eye. Some art-people even act smug, surrounded by the paraphernalias of machines, graphs, and charts, about the increasing degree of accuracy in their craft.

But, contrary to the intention, however, this scientific detection in art authenticity only proves the *opposite* of what it is supposed to prove, that is, that art is real, for it only proves that art is not real. By allowing itself to be authenticated now by science and technology, art has taken one gigantic step in proving its own hoax-ness.

Lawrence Jeppson tells of an art runner who had a (17th century) Jan Steen copied and, saying how good the copy looked, had the copier's name signed over Jan Steen's name as it appeared on the original and the copy. The customs office of the United States into which the art runner was entering was "tipped off" about a Jan Steen being brought in disguised as a copy apparently to avoid the 20 percent duty on all imported paintings. The customs officials, anticipating a "real" Jan Steen disguised as a copy, duly inspected the painting. When the copier's name was removed, there appeared "Jan Steen" underneath. Having thus been exposed as a "real" Jan Steen, the painting was charged the $28,000 customs duty. But the art runner now had the official blessing of owning a "real" Jan Steen, which he sold promptly for $50,000 within three days. "Today," observed Jeppson, "a twentieth-century Steen would go down to a crashing defeat *in the laboratory*." (Underline mine) Well, one forged painting might have gone down to a crashing defeat, but that small victory would be a bigger defeat for the whole art establishment. Just think: Only *in the laboratory* could they tell whether a forged Jan Steen was real or forged!

Consider as a simple fact of refutation that the notion of collectible art is wholly, absolutely, and exclusively *visual*. There is absolutely nothing in art that cannot be *seen* by bare human eyes. The original painter painted it with his bare eyes, with no mechanical help. There is no value in collectible art that cannot be gathered by visual inspection alone. *Everything* about the painting is right on the canvas and nowhere else. Why is science necessary to see what is all on the canvas and nowhere else?

Consider also this fact. If there were no "art market," no collection and possession, no art ownership as personal property, and so on, the common facts of a capitalist society, we wouldn't even have or need art "experts," any more than we would have or need "love experts." On the other hand, we *would* need love experts if love, especially "real love," were sold, bought, collected, possessed as exclusive private property. Or else, who would identify for us which love is real and which isn't but the experts? Yet, if this were the case, we would no longer speak of "falling in love." Instead, we would be speaking of "correct love," or "expert-certified love," "auction-house-guaranteed love," "refundable love," "scientifically-proven love," and so on. If only an art expert has to authenticate art, similarly, then it is no longer art.

Not unlike in love, in collectible art one's response is "emotional," not "scientific," "technical," or "logical." Like love, art cannot be forced onto a person's consciousness by either logic, science, or machine. In love, one instinctively "feels" or doesn't feel it; in art, one merely looks at an artwork and intuitively "feels" about the object of his inspection. A viewer of art would no more think about coming to the art gallery armed with an X-ray machine or a carbon-dating instrument or a chemical-analysis kit than would a lover with a similar paraphernalia on his first date. For, in either case, the introduction of science would be tantamount to confessing the falseness as well as the emptiness of the purpose: It would only show that one is interested in something other than art or love. Whatever that something is that one is interested in, it certainly isn't art or love, although that is what the claim is.

Art that cannot be judged solely by its artistic merit alone, of course, by looking at it, is no longer art and should not be called art. For all the factors that science proves—authenticity, age, identity—have *nothing* to do with art, but everything to do with the *material* which was used in the artwork, or with *fact* if the concern is the signature. A scientific analysis of the blue that La Tour supposedly used on Artwork X shows that the paint actually consisted of the ingredients that were native to the time and place of La Tour's life. Or, an X-ray shows that there was nothing else under the surface of Artwork X, thus proving that the painting on the canvas was apparently the only and therefore real one.

Although these scientific checks have been carefully anticipated by the forger, especially in the case of Van Meegeren's Vermeers, to defeat the probing scientists, such technical probings, even where they are useful, prove nothing about art itself, but only about the art material used in art. What is proved by the fact that Artwork X used the 17th century colors or that there is no other painting under the present one? Such scientific proofs say nothing about the artistic or aesthetic merits of art. It is not unlike trying to prove that Jane's name was really Susan, or that X-rays of her teeth show her age as twenty-one, in an effort to decide one's love for her. We cannot imagine the state of the collector's heart when he triumphantly confesses his love for Artwork X at the moment science proves its authenticity, any more than we can of the lover when he confesses his love for her upon scientific proofs of her name and age.

Scientific intervention in art authenticity comes about only *after* visual judgement has failed to identify the artwork's artistic authenticity and only *when* all aesthetic opinions regarding the work have disagreed with each other as to its art-ness. That science has to come into the controversy simply means that visual judgment and aesthetic opinions have proven to be insufficient to determine the work's art-ness or non-artness. But, why are visual judgment and aesthetic opinions insufficient, even if they are in disagreement? Whenever a scientist, not art connoisseur, pronounces the "real-ness"—and therefore "art-ness"—of this artwork or that, it painfully reminds all of us that something is terribly wrong with the art world. For each such pronouncement only proves the emptiness and nothingness of art itself.

All of art lies in the visual and aesthetic, not in the age of the canvas or the frame, not in the correct chemical ingredients of the colors used, not in the correctness of the signature on the canvas, but in what one *sees* in the picture, in the same way *all* of love lies in how one *feels*, not in the birth certificate or X-rays. No scientific analysis, for that matter, has ever produced proof that Artwork **X** is either good or bad art. The art-forgery identity is neither a logical issue—which is impossible in art—, nor a scientific one—which is irrelevant to art. It is an aesthetic one, the subjective-emotive-cultural judgment of anyone who views art. Every artwork is taken or ignored as a *whole,* and the whole must be taken into one's visual consciousness. One never looks at the name, the color ingredients, the price tag, or one segment of the whole, unless one's interest is in something other than art. No true lover would ask for a birth certificate or a chest X-ray from his prospective partner as a way of deciding his feelings toward her.

Once forgeries are identified as forgeries, art experts and scientists tend to make a big deal out of the supposed "differences." In fact, based on such differences, many experts "advise" people on how to tell the difference between a real one and a fake. But such a contrast is both silly and useless. It is silly because such a triumphant set of differences is entirely an after-the-fact accomplishment, once the fact of forgery has been *known.* The knowledge never existed *before* the discovery to help anyone who wants to know what is real and what is not. If such knowledge were possible, there would hardly be any forgeries to speak of. It is normally the chest-beating of a red-faced expert who triumphantly shouts to the world that he can tell the differences between real art and fakery. But, alas, only after the fact, not before.

Such a list of differences is also useless because we cannot apply them to other yet-unknown forgeries. The knowledge does not lead to the discovery of other forgeries because every forgery is different. For example, Hope B. Werness has listed the "differences" between real Vermeers and Van Meegeren's Vermeers, now that it is known that some of Vermeers are by Van Meegeren. She says that Vermeer's stylistic development is consistent and Van Meegeren's is not; the former's color has characteristic luminosity and the latter's lacks it; the former's texture is fully explored and the latter's is unnaturally smooth; the former's composition and space is clear-cut and the latter's congested and compressed; the former's value contrast shows subtle gradations and the latter's relatively unsubtle gradations; the former's works show accuracy and the latter's inaccuracy; the former's atmosphere is serene and the latter's nothing mysterious or subtle, etc.

Now, what are we to make of the differences listed above? Does that mean all the characteristics of Vermeer make good art in *all* other instances? Are we to march forward, armed with the knowledge about all good art and all fake art, looking to apply the standards that Werness has set down for us? How do any such differences apply to other instances? Can she herself, now in possession of such knowledge, discover all the fakes that exist in the art world?

Consider, finally, the fact that all such "differences" would have never been possible, Hope B. Werness's astuteness notwithstanding, if fate, not astute art expertise or science, had not intervened. The Van Meegeren-Vermeers were "discovered" only after Van Meegeren was arrested for having sold a Dutch treasure—his *own* Vermeer, that is—to the Nazis, which forced him to confess his forgeries. But even *after* his confession and extensive scientific analysis, many experts died still convinced that at least "some" Vermeers by Van Meegeren were *real* Vermeers. If Werness had been there at the scene in the mid-40s in Holland, could she have noticed all such glaring differences that set fake Vermeers apart from real Vermeers? None of the Vermeer experts then living could do it.

After some knowledge has thus been gained about what is supposed to be "real art," we are left with the uneasy feeling about "unreal art," or forgeries. They constitute at least one-half of all artworks in circulation, and they must be as good as the real stuff to mingle so successfully with the real ones. Other than their "negative" contribution of exposing the absurd illogic of real art, what can we say about them that is "positive" and useful?

Let's turn our attention to that aspect.

Chapter 16

The Master Is Dead

We may recall a comment made earlier about the ubiquitous desire people have when they come upon a wonderful work of art. People want to share their art experience with other people. When they read a good book and hear a good symphony, they want other people to read it and hear it too. Although this desire for art to be universally distributed is mostly confined to uncollectible art for the simple reason of its easy availability, it is also true of collectible art to some extent. It is only that the idea of private possession obscures this basic desire in everyone who encounters art.

This desire—universal and ubiquitous—is also true of *artists* themselves with their artworks. Virtually every artist wants his art—be it music, literature, painting, drama, sculpture, philosophy, what have you—to *spread* to the largest possible audience. A composer wants everyone to have an opportunity to hear his composition; a writer wants his novel to be on everyone's reading list; the painter wants his pictures to hang where everyone can see it, and so on. It would be highly unnatural and against our historical experience, although not wholly absent, for an artist to hide his artworks away from public appreciation. All artists want the applause—the single most important measure in the meaning of life for an artist—from the largest crowd that can appreciate their art. To be ignored by the public, more than being scorned, for his art is perhaps the most painful experience that an artist can endure.

It is for this reason that every painter is so anxious to have an exhibition of his artworks—the economic motive, while significant as a basic necessity of life, still being secondary. Van Gogh himself would be the one most upset with the fact that his "Irises" was purchased by a corporate collector at such a prohibitive sum that now it is practically hidden away from public viewing. If there were a choice between a large audience for one's artwork at smaller economic gains and a smaller audience at larger economic gains, I believe all non-market artists would gladly choose the former. The essence of all art, either from the public's reaction or from the artist's own inclination, is that it must spread to the widest circle possible.

But it is in the peculiar shortcomings and nature of collectible art, so irretrievably tied to collection and ownership, that it cannot spread to a wider audience in the way uncollectible art can through inexpensive copies and repeated performances. Only in collectible art is the artwork, no matter how famous, limited to one person, one institution, one spot, and one original as its sole representative. As well known as its author is, a Van Gogh sitting in a corporate vault, in an exclusive personal collection, or in a museum away from the rest of the world has no real value to anyone outside that circle. If any artwork can be said to be useless, it is the artwork that is exclusively privatized in someone's possession, there being no legitimate copies with which the work can spread. Art of this kind doesn't do anybody any good, least of all the artist himself whose instinct is for a wider distribution of his art.

Collected art, thus, goes against the basic inclination of art lovers everywhere and the obvious natural motive of all artists. But, how do we spread an artwork that is limited to one original in each instance at least in theory, no copies being available that are comparable in quality with the original, so that more people can enjoy the pleasure of art that the artwork represents?

Here is our place to reintroduce forgery, now in a substantially different, "positive" light. Let's consider forgery, the forger, and the artwork that is being forged, therefore, through a new perspective. We may find certain things that are fairly interesting about them and their interrelations.

All forgers, by definition, are extremely talented people. But their talent is limited generally to one thing: That is, *imitating* the masters whose style they choose to imitate. Their talent is almost wholly imitative, not creative or original. None of the celebrated forgers—Dossena, Van Meegeren, Elmyr de Hory, Keating, Stein, Wacker, and others—, even after their notoriety gained from forgery, ever succeeded on their own as artists. As their spectacular fame as forgers faded, so did the public interest in their *own* artworks. Although Tom Keating enjoyed some legitimate attention as an artist, having his own art-instruction program on BBC, that success, owing entirely to his notoriety as a forger, was neither large nor sustainable. For one reason or another, their talent in imitation is as spectacular as their talent as independent artists is meager. I suppose some people are simply more skilled in imitating known styles than creating their own.

In fact, skilled is an understatement. It is extraordinary in many ways that the forger's talent in imitating a Michelangelo, Van Gogh, or Picasso, whatever these masters' original talent may be, comes close enough to the comparable level of these masters themselves. Now, aside from the legal and moral implications, speaking in purely aesthetic terms, this is no mean achievement. The great accolades that are heaped on their forgeries as masterworks—that is, *before* their discovery as forgeries— simply demonstrate their phenomenal talent. Let's consider two examples, those of Alceo Dossena and David Stein, to refresh our memory of forging talent.

The quality of Dossena's works is described thusly by Frank Arnau in his book, *The Art of the Faker: Three Thousand Years of Deception*: "Collectors, art historians and dealers all paid homage to these treasures [Dossena's fakes], which gave evidence of true greatness. In accordance of their relative merits, they found new homes in famous museums and private collections...Many authorities expatiated upon their knowledge of the masters and schools to which they unhesitatingly ascribed these sculptures." Arnau also reports the description by a German art expert who observed post-forgery Dossena at work: "We had witnessed the reincarnation of a Renaissance master...at once alarming and enthralling thought. One of the fundamental laws governing our attitude to all art seems to have lost its meaning, the law according to which a work of art can only originate once...."

Then there is a description of Stein's talent for copying modern masters, originally appearing in the *Daily Telegraph Magazine* and quoted in Robert Wraight's book *The Art Game, Again*: "In the most frantic day of his career he sold to a New York dealer at one o'clock in the afternoon three Chagall watercolors that had not been painted when he arose at 6 a.m. In the space of seven hours Stein had aged the paper with tea, invented subjects, executed the works in quick succession, dashed to a framer for a while-you-wait job, zipped on to a photographer for photostats of the pictures, run back to the studio to forge certificates of authentication and kept his appointment with the dealer with a few minutes to spare." For these particular forgeries Stein received $10,500.

(Not being able to make it on his own, of course, Dossena died in a pauper's hospital, which is quite similar to the fate visited upon most forgers after their unmasking. Understandably, the art establishment has been harsh on forgers, attributing many unsavory personality traits to them as it ascribes highly uncomplimentary terms to their post-discovery artworks. Often forgers are described as low-life liars, displaying poor character and unstable mentality. But, of course, there is no evidence to support the view that the forgers are in general any worse human beings than the better-known artists—such as Whistler, Rothko, Van Gogh, Gauguin, or even Rembrandt, the paragon of moral integrity, according to his 1988 biography by Gary Schwartz who described the artist as having "a nasty disposition and an untrustworthy character"— and their artworks, if the forgeries are included, are, according to experts, some of the greatest the world has ever seen.)

On the other hand, the relationship between the masters whose works are copied and forged and the forgers who copy and forge them is somewhat more curious and complex than we normally suppose. With few exceptions, forgers in general are far from being the hard-boiled, coldly-calculating professional bandits who only mechanically master the technique and singularly for monetary gains. To the man, the forgers claim a special sense of uncommon "one-ness" and affinity with the masters whose works they copy. This is not surprising in view of the inordinate amount of time and effort they spend studying the styles, characteristics, and psychology of the masters as part of their trade.

Equally unsurprising is that the forgers eventually emerge as authorities on the masters they copy and know so much about. Tom Keating's BBC program was actually about how to imitate the masters he had forged. It was his view that "The forger is much more intimate with the master than the expert." At the time of Van Meegeren's completion of his first forgery of Vermeer, there was no one in the world who was as thoroughly knowledgeable about Vermeer's technique as Van Meegeren himself.

The ways in which they describe their special "relationship" with the masters they copy are quite interesting.

Keating: "I couldn't paint a Goya, Rembrandt or even a Samuel Palmer for a million pounds or to save my life. But when the spirit of a long-dead artist comes into my hands the images flow out on to the canvas without the slightest effort on my part. I am not a spiritualist and I have never dabbled in the occult; I cannot account for the strange thing that happens to me and will not try."

At one time Keating recalled that Degas painted a self-portrait "through" his hand. "It sounds ridiculous, I know, but Degas really did draw that picture through me and many others besides. I woke up one morning and found it on the easel, in place of the scratchy, silly daub that I'd been working on the day before: a pastel self-portrait of the artist in a hat, completely unmistakable in form and technique." (As told to Norman)

Robert Wraight describes David Stein: "It was essential for him to get inside the soul and mind of the [master] artist before he could forge a particular man's work."

Here is the summary of the meticulous way Van Meegeren "became" Vermeer while in preparation to do his first Vermeer: "He had steeped himself so thoroughly in the master's technique that what he had assiduously memorized had now become an integral part of his own store of knowledge... He had become the *medium* of the man whom he wished to imitate... Increasingly obsessed with an urge to attain the unattainable, he took refuge in the mental transformation of Han van Meegeren into a resurrected Vermeer. He ceased to draw a distinction between reality and appearance. The boundaries between them had dissolved." (Told by Arnau. Underline is mine.)

Asked during the trial why he continued to forge Vermeers after the first one, he replied: "I enjoyed painting them so much. One comes to a condition in which one is no more master of oneself." Reporting on this, Laurie Adams observed that "Van Meegeren was implying that he had lost control of himself and was not entirely responsible for his actions."

What does all this mean? What are we to make of the forgers who (1) are extraordinarily talented in imitation of certain masters whose works cannot spread to wider audiences in the limited number of originals; (2) know more about the masters than anyone, to the extent of claiming to have merged into one with them, yet their talent and knowledge about the masters cannot be put to publicly useful functions; and (3) are, just as extraordinarily, failures on their own as artists, dismissed and scorned by the art world, and fading out from history generally in misery and disgrace?

Switching our mental gear and looking at the forgers from a wholly different but "positive" perspective because our old way of looking at forgery doesn't help us that much, what can we say about them? In a bold new perspective, this is what we can say: FORGERS ARE THE LIVING INSTRUMENT OF THE DEAD MASTERS.

In other words, forgers are the masters' helpers who can continue to produce the works the masters, obviously on the account of their death, can no longer paint but *would have*, had they lived longer. Forgers merely *finish* what the dead masters would have done had they continued to live and produce. Whatever the masters created that made them famous masters, thanks to forgers, is continuing through their forgeries.

There are obviously many objections arising from this new perspective on forgery, and we will try to meet them as we go along.

First, there is the problem of "originality" representing the master's creative life. Can the forger maintain the level of the master's originality and creativity? The answer to this question, hence the solution to the problem of originality, would be that the forger *never* claims credit for the master's originality and creativity, although we have seen that much of the master's so-called originality is bunk, for much is repeated over and over after one particular, perhaps original style. After all, the forger is a "forger." He never claims to *be* the master himself. He is merely the living agent of the dead master who can no longer paint himself, although he would have mostly in the style that he had developed and was familiar with had he lived longer.

Second, there is the problem of "quality." Would a forged Van Gogh be as good as a real Van Gogh? This problem can be left up to art experts to solve and, from what we have seen especially in the case of Wacker's Van Goghs, it appears that quality is largely a matter of personal opinion. Concerning one of the essential ingredients of quality, some philosophers have argued that forgeries are not real artworks because they lack the "spirit of the age" in which they were conceived and executed. In other words, modern forgeries reflect today's attitudes and prejudices, not those of the original time. This objection, however, can be met in the following two ways:

One, the forger is so deeply immersed in the master he is copying that the master and the forger become *one* and the *same*, and the latter can feel the master's whole personality working through his hand. Although there is some element of fantasy-like quality in their various immersion accounts, especially in Keating's, I believe them to be telling the truth. Anyone who has attempted a serious fiction or has acted in the "method" mold of acting can understand this idea of total immersion.

Two, the forgery is so good in quality that the spirit-of-the-age issue becomes a moot one. Or, even when the forgery is not as good as the master's own, say being only "90 percent good," the difference matters very little or, when it does matter, only to the extent of the difference in quality. If a forgery is 90 percent as good as the original, according to the master's standards, then the forgery is worth exactly 90 percent of the original's value. Why is a 90 percent-good artwork unacceptable to the art world, which sometimes sells and buys that which is practically zero-percent good, like the empty canvas or the shovel? I would personally take a 90-percent-good fake Michelangelo than a 100-percent genuine nothing. Moreover, how can we say that a small difference—10 percent—makes one artwork *nothing* because it is a forgery, and the other one *everything* because it is an original? In some cases, to complicate the issue, forgeries were considered "better" than the originals. Clifford Irving tells of the cases where Elmyr de Hory's forgeries, mixed on purpose with genuine ones, were submitted to the French government-certified experts; they approved the forgeries as genuine and rejected the genuine ones as forgeries!

Third, those who were and are critical of Van Meegeren's Vermeers, as we have seen, are actually critical of Van Meegeren, *not* Vermeer. While Van Meegeren *was* being Vermeer, everyone praised him. Now that he is no longer Vermeer, but actually Van Meegeren posing as Vermeer, everyone jumps on him and finds all sorts of flaws in his pretended Vermeers as was the case in the Werness article quoted earlier. But by all accounts, Van Meegeren should have never *existed*, for as far as the artworks were concerned only Vermeer existed, and how they all loved him! To the extent that they were and are taken as Vermeers, thus, criticizing them *as* Van Meegeren is both hypocritical and incorrect. A forger should be criticized only if he does a *poor* job of forging a master. But that creates a small dilemma of its own: Perfect forgery vs. poor forgery.

We will solve the dilemma this way. Let's say the forger does a perfect job and, therefore, no one notices the difference; so, here there is no problem. Let's say, on the other hand, the forger does a poor job and, therefore, everyone notices the difference; so here there is no problem.

A forger cannot be criticized for *being* a forger. Why should he be punished for adding more Van Goghs, more Michelangelos, more Pollocks than there would have been, as long as these artworks are deemed valuable? If these masterworks are good, why aren't *more* of them even *better*? Who would criticize someone for having created a "Tenth Symphony" by Beethoven if everyone agrees that it *should* have been Beethoven's own "Tenth" had he lived longer? There is not a single reason to condemn forgers for having created more of the masters' artworks long after they are gone. Now, that a forger sells his forgeries and enriches himself, as in the case of Van Meegeren, is an altogether different story and requires a practical solution for that problem alone. But in the *very act* of continuing to produce more of masterworks than there would otherwise have been itself, there should be nothing but praise and honor, not misery and disgrace. What if the fabulous talents of the above-mentioned forgers were *encouraged* and were taken advantage of in a way benefiting the public, instead of being dismissed and condemned, at the height of their talent? What if Wacker were supported and encouraged to produce more Van Goghs, Keating more Palmers, Van Meegeren more Vermeers, Dossena more Renaissance art, and Stein more Chagalls?

Would the deceased artists mind? Very likely not, inferring from the way Picasso reacted to forgeries. He said he always signed his name on forgeries if he thought they were good enough to have been his own. Personally, if I thought someone could continue to produce ideas and works just like me after my own death, as if I myself continued to live and work, I would indeed be grateful to the living instrument of the ideas and works that I didn't get to finish or produce within my own life span.

Let's suppose, just to broaden our horizon still more, that a scientist developed a way of producing artificially a certain variety of grain that is highly sought after. Agricultural experts swear that there is no difference between the artificial grain and the natural grain. Consider these two facts: (1) the grain is highly sought after as useful to mankind; and (2) experts cannot tell them apart. Should we honor the scientist with a Nobel prize or condemn him to misery and disgrace, and possibly a jail term for having invented the new grain? For the scientist to be condemned for his talent, either of the two conditions must be met, both of which obviously cannot: First, we must say that the grain is not really that useful, which is a lie simply because it is a multibillion dollar business. Second, we must say that the artificial grain is not as good as the original, which is a contradiction of experts who are the only ones who know the difference. The art establishment, if this grain-analogy holds true, seems, for reasons that have nothing to do with art, to be the only institution in society that cannot tolerate more of good things.

The only factor not figured in the above hypothesis is the market. The grain *market*, of course, is a different matter wholly unrelated either to the usefulness of the grain or to the realness of the new substitute. Likewise, the art *market* is unrelated to either the desirability of spreading art universally or the goodness of artworks that are produced outside their approved channel.

Perhaps we are talking logic and commonsense that is too outrageous to the art market. The art market, where huge sums exchange hands for artworks, operates on its own rules and assumptions, however illogical and in violation of commonsense they may be.

Art forgery is nothing like any other forms of forgery, fakery or duplicity. It is the only forgery that has no victims. It only multiplies its beneficence each time one is produced and finds a receptive home. Dealers have a larger volume of traffic with masterworks to sell. Artists can earn a decent living on the side doing forgeries, if not exclusively. Collectors can collect their beloved masterworks at cheaper prices. The public can have easy access to such masterworks at local museums or even at their own homes. And for the masters themselves, happiest of them all with this increased spreading of their works, their reputation can only grow and become more universal. Thus, it is entirely possible to view forgeries from less than a negative point of view as we have been accustomed to.

So, what should be our next step to take concerning the so-called forgeries?

Chapter 17

Long Live the Extensions!

Before we can fit our new conception of forgeries into the existing market scheme of things, let's first examine the mechanism of art demand and art supply itself.

The art market is really a misnomer, a contradiction in terms. I am not implying here the "moral" principle of selling art that outrages some liberal people who believe that art should not be sold or bought. Rather, I am referring to its pure market modus operandi. For, incidentally, I don't see anything wrong with selling and buying artworks as long as such selling and buying is merely means to an end, the end being the appreciation of art itself. After all, artists have to live and it costs to produce or perform artworks, and the market is the chief means by which all great works of art find their audiences worldwide.

What I mean by it is that the art market is neither about art, nor, strictly speaking, about market. We have already seen that art has nothing to do with what is sold and bought as art. Now, we need to look at the "market," which, while being fairly different, presumes to be part of the conventional market form with which we are familiar.

Although it claims to operate on the basis of the principle of market economy—demand-supply, auction, price—the art market is closer to a model of monopoly than a marketplace. If a free, open market is based on the unceasing workings of demand and supply, and the auctioning process of price-determination between the two elements, the art market is hardly the "marketplace" it claims to be. It claims that it is a marketplace where buyers demand and sellers supply, but in practice its supply is strictly limited while demand is ever on the increase. The consequence of this imbalance is the multiplying price for the limited pool of supplies in masterworks and hot-selling living artists. Existing masterworks are in short supply because they cannot increase their number, while contemporary living artists are selectively reduced by the necessity of a fewer-the-better principle of the art market. In a strange way, we might say of the art market what Thomas Malthus said about population: Demand increases geometrically (1,2,4,8,16,32,64...) whereas supply increases arithmetically (1,2,3,4,5,6,7...) at the art marketplace.

Even Adam Smith, the first articulate voice of our market economy, was somewhat puzzled by the place of art in the market economy. Like a precious gem, art has no utilitarian value or function that can be precisely measured in monetary units. As a commodity, not unlike a gem, art's value—not "artistic value," for Adam Smith was already thinking of art as a commodity even then—rests solely on the fact that it is rare. But the similarities between art and gems end here. Several thoughts that separate gems from artworks come to mind, which give us a better grasp of the art market.

First, a precious gem may be rare in the sense that it cannot be found in large numbers by virtue of their rareness in nature, and its number is thus limited accordingly. A "rare" work of art, on the other hand, is kept rare by *artificially* limiting the production of more such artworks, as a result of which rare artworks wouldn't be rare any more. Unlike the rare gem, even rare artworks *can* be produced, as has been seen in reality, in any desired number by the simple process of forgery. Forgery may have many legal, cultural, psychological implications in the term itself, but one thing about it is certain: It produces master artworks. But the strenuous legal enforcement against forgeries, and all the attendant moral scorn from art-people and the holier-than-thou attitude shown by the art establishment toward forgery makes sure that this unlimited production of rare artworks never materializes.

Second, the price of a rare gem is determined by the fact of its rarity vis a vis the desire for it expressed in the size of the demand and the difficulty associated with its production in finding it. But the issue in art prices is complicated by the fact that the commodity is also called "art," with all the non-market nuances implied in the term. A lover of precious gems and stones need not explain or defend himself to the world for his love of those items. There is neither explanation nor defense necessary in his desire for and acquisition of them strictly as market commodities. But a "lover of art" is not a gem collector; nor is art the same as a gem. Unlike the precious rare gem for the exclusive pleasure of its owner, art is regarded as open to *all* mankind. A lover of gems would be reluctant to wear the title "lover of gems" with any distinction, for nothing terribly distinguished—perhaps only embarrassment for its hedonistic implication—is included in gem-loving and gem-collecting. A lover of art, on the other hand, is an honorable title and is often mistaken for a philanthropist, one who gives generously to charity, although art-collecting and giving to charity have nothing in common in reality. Lovers of art, indeed, would be the first to argue that there can be no price placed on art—only love, respect, and honor.

Third, the result of interplay between the first two factors (artificially limited numbers and philanthropy-charity associated with art collection), obviously, is two-fold: An intentionally reduced supply, with geometrically increasing demand created by the new affluence and fashion in art collection, and unabated increases in price for so-called art lovers. Art price, of all prices placed on goods and services, however, is the most puzzling of all prices simply because of the peculiar nature of art-production. In short, it takes so *little* to produce one. Often, as in the empty canvas and the shovel, it takes *nothing* at all to produce an artwork. Van Gogh's "Irises" was sold for a record price of 50 million dollars and much more if taxes, auctioneer's fees, and other overheads were included. But how was the price determined? How was that price derived for a canvas with some wild colors and figures of irises whose effect is less than a moving picture of the same subject and whose realism is less than photography? In response, we could say that the workings of demand and supply, and the process of open auction are in place to insure that the price conformed to the rules of the marketplace. This response, however, applies to *all* commodities sold on the market, *not* to art as commodity. In real practice, the price of the Van Gogh, and indeed the prices of all artworks for that matter, is an exceedingly difficult one to determine. Why?

If we consider the marketplace and its pricing principle, we know that the art prices do not follow the market pricing principle because it is not an "open" market. The art market is a monopoly market where its demand and supply do not come to a free, open interplay of production and competition. When there is only one work called the "Irises," there is no way we can speak of fair market price.

If we consider its "artistic value," as we have seen earlier, the "Irises" is in a difficult position because, like all other collectible artworks in existence, it has never been subjected to the pure artistic judgment which only history can render. Historical judgment is made neither by the experts' pronouncement, nor by the whims of the public. Historical judgment is an unceasing process, filtered and readjusted through different generations, to shape the final resting ground of each artwork. But the "Irises" has never been open to that sort of historical process. Rather, it has always occupied the rarefied and somewhat restricted elite chamber of high society and art collection. The work has never been made universally available in large numbers to the general public at a reasonable price that anyone can afford to say that its present judgment is a historical one.

If we consider its labor value—which is what Adam Smith had in mind—, on the other hand, the issue is still more complicated. The labor theory of value postulates that the price of a commodity is represented in the time of labor it took to produce it. But, what is the worth of an artist's one-hour's labor, one-day's labor, or one-month's labor in a more general sense of compensation? One of the paintings by Modern Artist Jasper Johns, who is still living, has recently been sold for five million dollars. How long did he work to complete the painting? One hour? One day? One week? If it is indeed difficult to assess the value on paintings, where does *that* price come from? While answers to such questions are perhaps impossible to get and perhaps too futile to try, one thing is certain: If cheaper copies were universally available, such an obviously outrageous price would have never been possible. Were reasonable copies available, we can be sure, the Van Gogh or Johns would have been settled on its *natural* price.

Then, what is the natural price of a painting and how does it come about? The natural price of a commodity, according to classic political economy, is one that is arrived at when there is no tampering with either the demand or supply of a particular commodity. In art, it is possible only when demand is met by a universally available supply of goods in demand. The price one pays to see a play by Shakespeare, to buy the recording of a symphony by Beethoven, or to get a copy of Plato's books is the natural price, arrived at by the untempered demand and supply of the marketplace. Thus, natural price is possible only when neither demand nor supply is artificially restricted. In the case of collectible art, the restrictions placed on supply artificially determine the artworks's price in a monopolistic fashion. Unlike the rare gem, the rareness of the Johns or the Van Gogh is a condition created by the art market, not intrinsic to the artwork itself, an artificial one that hinges on the insistence that no copies ever be produced. Obviously, this is a condition peculiar only to collectible art, for copies and repeated performances are made out of all great uncollectible works of art. The natural price, as well as the historical position, of such artworks would be possible *only if* the artworks under consideration could be supplied in unlimited numbers—supplemented by an unlimited production of copies or forgeries, WHOSE LIMITATION WOULD BE DETERMINED ONLY BY THE EXTENT OF DEMAND ITSELF.

This practice has only been partially in operation at the marketplace. As it stands today, forgeries have increased the volume of the artworks that are in supply by making it twice as large as it would have otherwise been. In other words, we have twice as many masterworks or works by the masters because of the forgeries in circulation. Thousands of valued artworks are hung in museums and kept in private collections only because of forgeries. But the production of such extra supplies, as forgeries, has been conducted under rather adverse circumstances, struggling against legal restrictions as well as general prejudice toward forgeries. Why couldn't the volume increase further, to "supplement an insufficient supply," to quote art dealer David Gould's explanation for the Tom Keating phenomenon?

In the less circumspect world of commercialism, this supplementing of insufficient supplies of goods and services in demand is far more straightforward, if not blatant. Consider the sequel to "Gone With the Wind" mentioned earlier. Although its author Margaret Mitchell has long been dead, her heirs have decided to *continue* her work *through* the hands of her "forger," as if she never died. Responding to the continuing public demand for "more" Margaret Mitchell, the heirs and their professional agents looked high and low to find the best "living instrument" of the dead author. Upon finding the best "forger" in the persona of a Virginian (her name is not important because it will be Margaret Mitchell's story and characters), the publisher paid close to five million dollars even before one single word had been written for "Gone With the Wind II." But who cares? If a new Van Gogh were found, would art collectors want to know about the "quality" of the painting first? No. To them, that it bears the name Van Gogh is good enough. To the public, the name Margaret Mitchell's "Gone With the Wind" is good enough. Can we call the Virginian woman a forger? Yes, because that's what she exactly is. Newspaper columnist Tom Wicker has actually called the sequel a "fake novel" because its author is not Mitchell, but he is just being too technical. Do we condemn the fake-Margaret Mitchell to misery, disgrace, and possible jail? No. Thanks to our commercialism, not pretensions to art, the faker will be getting a handsome fee, perhaps in the millions, for her forgery. This sequel phenomenon has been true, though less spectacularly, for Sherlock Holmes many years after Sir Arthur Conan Doyle's death (the forgers: Nicholas Myers, John Gardner) and James Bond many years after Ian Flemming's death (the faker: John Gardner), as well as in such lesser cases as "Blondie," "Ann Landers," and others.

Why can't there be "sequels," *many* of them since it's much easier to produce in large numbers, to the master collectibles? Why not more Michelangelos, more Van Goghs, more Picassos, and so on as there are more of but less-important Scarlett O'Haras, Holmes, and Bonds? If it is good to produce more of Mitchell, Doyle and Flemming, why wouldn't it be good to have more of Michelangelos, Van Goghs, Picassos, and so on, as long as their artworks are in demand as Mitchell's and the others' apparently are. In fact, there is so much demand for artworks that even a living artist's work is sold at millions of dollars. If so-called lovers of art protest that we cannot do sequels to artworks because they are "art," I would respond by saying that it is *all the more reason* to do sequels, and in unlimited numbers. A Michelangelo in every household would certainly be better than a Mitchell in every household, a Van Gogh better than a Doyle, a Picasso better than a Flemming, and so on, if we are to believe in the exorbitant prices paid to their artworks. If these art lovers truly loved art, as they say they do, then, there should be no qualms about spreading what they so dearly love to every household, if possible, in the glory of art.

Obviously, that is not happening, at least not officially and with the blessings of the art establishment. While their operation is much more "commercial" than the art-less and unscrupulous commercial world, their claim to art and art-loving gives the art market a respectable shield behind which to hide. The lifeblood of art is undoubtedly its "collectibility" and all the psychological, cultural, and economic elements the collectibility implies. Remove that collectibility, and the art market—and perhaps art itself—would simply collapse. Aside from interior decoration, illustrative art, and artsy-craftsy uses of pretty things, I doubt very much that people would pay that much attention to this, that or the other artwork which reputedly sells for millions. If the collectibility-possession factor were removed from art and the fabulous millions the latter commands, the public's attention to what is collectible art today would amount to no more than pretty pictures on calendars, or beautiful but commonplace sunsets, clouds, and flowers. It is, then, this collectibility that forces the art market to do the most art-hating thing of all: IT KEEPS ART FROM BEING PUBLICLY BENEFICIAL BY MAKING IT UNAVAILABLE UNIVERSALLY. In the name of art, the art market keeps art from becoming universally available, loved, and enjoyed. In the name of love for art, so-called art lovers would want no one else to enjoy it. It is indeed every art collector's nightmare that one day art might become available to everyone through its unlimited production of identical copies and forgeries.

Of all the forgeries art forgery is the only form of forgery that is beneficial to everyone and harmful to no one. This is how Clifford Irving described Elmyr de Hory's self-justification as a forger: "Forging a Matisse or a Modigliani harmed no one. Had he stolen from a poor man with a wife and six children to support? Had he killed anyone? Was he an extortionist, a member of the Mafia? Certainly not, and accordingly he held his head high." What de Hory forgot to mention was his contribution to art and the number of Matisses and Modiglianis, among others, that he helped increase for the benefit of museums and private collections. He had good reason to be proud.

Consider the harmful effects of other forms of forgery. Faked historical documents distort historical truth; bogus currency disrupts the total amount of money in circulation and thereby the economy itself; forged checks amount to stealing someone else's money; poisonous food hurts and possibly kills people; imitation government documents threaten social order. None of these forms of forgery contributes anything positive to society while disrupting its order and institutions, and hurting individual lives. But, what harm can art forgery possibly cause? If a collector smugly looks at his art collections and is satisfied with the quality of the artworks, why does it matter if they are forgeries or if they are nothing—like the shovel and the empty canvas—as long as he is *satisfied?* The collector *never* expects anything from his art collections other than to *be there.* In fact, forgery in collectible art is the only form of forgery that can be repeated indefinitely without creating any social disruption or individual harm.

What a collector wants is the sense of *possession*. The *quality* of whatever he owns matters little or nothing to him, since he knows little or nothing about art and he cannot tell forgeries from real art. In fact, not even experts can. Big-time art collectors show remarkably little interest or knowledge or desire in *un*collectible art, such as literature, music, and philosophy. Unlike paintings and sculptures, these art forms are uncollectible and they require some active cultural and intellectual curiosity to acquire a taste for them, which these collectors almost totally lack. No personal image can be farther from the notion of culture and enlightenment than the image of the likes of Nelson Rockefellers and Algur Meadows. Fortunately for them, their lack of culture, intellectual curiosity, and other finer points of art does not interfere with collecting art. For art collection has nothing to do with art and culture, and everything to do with money and the market. It is the *ownership* that gives the collector his satisfaction. That's why it matters little or nothing *what* actually passes as art in his collections. Forgeries, as much as the universalization of art enjoyment by everyone at cheap prices, scare the collector to death precisely for that reason.

In sculpture reproductions are easier to make and hence more controversial. Many copies are made either by the heir or other unauthorized persons from recastings of the original. Why are recastings forgeries when they are identical with the original? The idea is that the copies were not *authorized* by the original sculptor. Of course, this is a technical point, not an artistic principle. The United States Bureau of Customs, for tax purpose, recognizes the first *six* castings as originals and any more as "unauthorized" forgeries. Why is the seventh casting any different from the sixth, or an eighth from the sixth, and so on? Sylvia Hochfield relates the difficulty involved in recastings by pointing out that bronze casts were made after his death from French sculptor Daumier's plaster figure titled "Ratapoil" although the sculptor "never intended the work to be cast in bronze." But reproductions in sculpture come closest to the universal distribution of cheap artworks without sacrificing quality.

In fact, art forgery is also a misnomer, a contradiction in terms. There is no such thing as art forgery, or forged art, only a forged signature. No art is so bad that it does not have *any* artistic value. If I pretended to be Michelangelo and put his signature on my painting, what I have is not art forgery, but a forged signature. One may claim that this is a rather technical distinction, and a picky one at that. No, it is not a technical distinction and its importance cannot be brushed aside. What I have done is to *pretend* to be someone that I am not. The artwork that I created must stand on its own as an artwork, regardless of what name it bears as its author. I may have only used Michelangelo's name in a fraudulent sense for my personal profit, but then the matter should be dealt with separately from my artwork's worth.

Thus, we can separate forged art from forgery itself, or art from the market. This can be done only when forgeries are produced by talented artists for the benefit of art and society, not for themselves or the art market or the collector. To do this, we need to create a new concept concerning art forgery, a concept that serves our appreciation of art far more than what we can glean from art books or from the media reports of fabulous deals made. Enjoying art this way is like enjoying Shakespeare from a theatre program or Beethoven from somebody's whistling; you can get an idea of what it is but never the full enjoyment. With the new concept, however, collectible art, like uncollectible art, will become universally enjoyable at reasonably cheap prices. Isn't it truly what art is all about?

We will call the new concept, in view of the true functions of forgery, "EXTENSION," the living extensions of the dead master, rather than forgery. With it, our whole notion of forgery also changes its meaning.

Chapter 18

The Art of Positive Painting

We are now in a position to think of forgery, or in its new form "extension," in a positive, vital, and dynamic light. All previous criticisms of forgery have treated it as forgery, not as extension, hence their primarily negative attitude toward it. Once we look at it as living extensions of masterworks, and once we are free from the obsessive notion of "collection" and ownership, we may find much that is wonderful about the new idea about art forgery.

Our first task, then, is to create out of forgery a certain set of principles for extensions. Let's call extensions a particular category of forgery, that is, some forgeries are thought to qualify as extensions. Those forgeries that do not qualify to be extensions shall be called "fakes." This way, we can say forgeries consist of two broad categories: EXTENSIONS AND FAKES. Accordingly, we should also have a new category called "extenders," those forgers who extend the masters' artworks in their respective styles and character.

Extensions are those artworks that qualify to be the continuing production of bygone masters; and fakes are those, for one reason or another, that fail to do so. These two categories are already part of the working arrangements of the art market. Not unlike the amnesty for all illegal aliens who are already in this country and have proven to be productive citizens, we are merely giving the forgeries their intellectual respectability, cultural legitimacy, and emotional support. Obviously, those forgeries that are already mingling with real masterworks, undetected of their true origin, are regarded as extensions of those masterworks by default. Those, for one reason or another, do not qualify by having been exposed to be forgeries are already branded as fakes and are treated accordingly. But since our introduction of the term extension is somewhat new, we should endeavor to make the distinction as clear as possible.

Extensions do not claim to be original works by the extender. They simply represent the continuing productivity of the dead master through the living hands of the extender. The master had already perfected his style and character to the extent that they are known to be his style and character. The extender simply continues the same style and character, only varying the subject matters as the master himself would have done. The role of the extender in the world of art and art appreciation should be absolutely minimal or, I should say, nonexistent. He is merely being the living instrument of the dead master, not the dead master himself. If the master could have programmed all his creative impulses into a capable computer before he died, the extender would be functioning pretty much like the computer, no more and no less. Criticizing the extender for pretending to be the master, as all critics of forgery have done, is as unfair as criticizing the computer for the same misbehavior. As long as he is an extender, not a faker, he might as well not exist at all. His mind is that of the master; his hands are those of the master; his eyes are those of the master, and so on, as many forgers have claimed to be the case. Now, why would this be a difficult concept to accept altogether?

We must set the extender apart from a faker who is really a common thief. To do so, the process in which the extender is to be chosen, masterworks to be extended selected, and the quality of workmanship to be extracted, and so on, must be established under strict planning and supervision. As something of half-extension and half-fakery, the copying of well-known masterworks—from real paintings and photographs of subjects—is already being done commercially, as in the case of Daniel Delamare's copy factory in Paris, which prices its products at 5000 to 20,000 dollars a piece. What needs to be done is making this sort of enterprise better planned and executed on a larger scale.

To be more specific, consider the following scenario.

First, the governing body of extension work will be formed, to consist of highly qualified art personnel: Museum directors, art critics, gallery owners and dealers, auction house officials, academic historians, and a host of other art experts. They will supervise all phases of personnel decision, art selection, and extension production.

Second, the governing body shall choose, by open and objective testing and consideration of experience and talent, as many artists as possible who are or can be trained to be excellent extenders. The best pool of such artists is, of course, found among the existing forgers, mostly in Europe. (For some reason Americans can't cut it in this business of tedious exactitude and immersion). These qualified extenders may choose to do extensions full-time or, if they wish to try some on their own, part-time, depending on their needs, inclinations, and ability. Those well known master forgers—in the caliber of de Horys, Keatings, Van Meegerens, Dossenas, and Steins—can serve as master teachers in instructing other extenders as well as in direct participation of extension production.

Third, the governing body of experts, upon being duly sworn to be conscientious and open-minded with their task, then shall examine the works as to their qualifications as "extensions." Now, any child can say that the extension is not the real one and, therefore, should be dismissed as a fake, since its fakery is already known. However, we must trust the unbiased judgment of the governing body of experts to fight this temptation to submit to their prejudice and foreknowledge, and declare them unqualified.

Fourth, those paintings now qualified to be certifiable extensions shall bear a mark of such identity somewhere to prevent them from falling into irrefutable hands. This mark of identity, but not that of the extender, must be small and known only to the extender and the governing body of experts.

Fifth, all extended works then shall first be distributed without comment to all schools, universities, museums, government offices, and any other such public conveniences where artworks may be displayed, and then to the general public upon demand. There should be a small charge for each extension, to cover the costs of production but nothing more. These public institutions and individuals, upon their own decisions, may request extensions by certain masters to fit their location or function.

Sixth, the qualified extenders shall get a reasonable compensation for their labor, but no more than the prevailing rates for cost of living. Any more than average living expenses paid to artists merely corrupt them and disrupt their work. Wealth may do many things, but it does not serve the purpose of art or artists.

Considering the relative simplicity of ideas expressed in each collectible art that currently exists, what remains to be done for the extender is to become familiar with the technique of the master in order to extend his works. Central ideas have already been created by the master, and extensions merely constitute their variations in subject matter. If Picasso left 3000 artworks, is there any reason why there shouldn't 30,000 or 300,000 of his works as long as the world likes his paintings? His reputation has already been established and there is nothing in extensions that can hurt it. The master had his genius in creating the style and character in his art, stamped with his originality and talent. The extender as an "invisible" technician, though a superb one, does not pretend to have inherited the master's genius, merely his technique.

In sculpture, of course, this extension process is not nearly as necessary because reproductions can be made precisely from the original. Its method of reproduction is somewhat easier than that in painting. But the controversy is not abated by the moral and ethical implications of reproductions, the same kind of controversy surrounding painting.

The principle of extension is just the same in sculpture, however. When criticized about his liberal reproduce-and-sell policy for some of his sculpture collections, Nelson Rockefeller was said to have been unequivocal about the righteousness of his position as he said: "I think it's wonderful!" He also maintained, in Pat Gilmour's account, that "His motive (apart from business, of course) was to *share his collections with people* by means of the most faithful facsimiles possible, since good art had now been priced out of almost everybody's reach." (Parentheses original. Underline mine.) Never mind that his copies, costing mostly in the thousands and reputed to be "indistinguishable from the originals," were still out of reach of most people. But the idea itself is similar to our extensions in painting.

Benefits from legitimate extensions are incalculable. The art market, the artist, and art itself will all benefit from more widely spread artworks than their current exclusion by wealth and number allows. The moral qualms—mainly the staple of art-people—, the economic consideration—mainly the concern of the art market—, and the cultural misgivings—mainly the sentiment of collectors—, are small prices to pay considering the vast benefits the extensions would confer upon all true lovers of art.

For the art market, the closed, monopolized market would open up to the true workings of demand and supply in art once this extension principle is put into effect. Would Van Gogh's "Irises" be as expensive as 50 million dollars if honest, open competition were allowed to enter the market? It is only when the market is open, both in demand and in supply, can we truly see each artwork's "real price" emerge. What would be the price of the "Irises" if its indistinguishable quality extensions, or even replicas, were available in virtually unlimited numbers and were allowed to enter the auction house? As for the market itself, selling thousands upon thousands of "Irises" at a reasonable price to the whole general public would spread the art business much more profitably than selling one copy for 50 million. Now, multiply that possibility with yet thousands upon thousands more. It makes perfect business sense as well to accept the idea of extensions. Can one imagine seeing an extension of the "Irises" in every household?

For the artist living or dead, the idea is extremely appealing since his main goal as an artist is to spread his artworks—or the ideas embodied in them—throughout the world and to posterity. Instead of his artworks being secluded in a corporate vault or private collection, they would be in every conceivable public institution and convenience, and in ordinary homes. His artistic reputation, already established, will only increase with this wider contact with and greater participation by the public. It is also good for the public, as M. Pabst Battin suggests, when "Copies of visual works—as well as those within music and literature—

will also civilize and make more profound the existence of the beholder. If so, it may be our obligation to give reliable copies as widespread distribution as possible, in the visual arts as we now do in music and literature." For that, Battin considers "Making not only practical but inexpensive exact, molecule-for-molecule replication of the great master." But of course, for the time being, until such high-technology becomes available, we should be satisfied with extensions.

For art itself, nothing could be better. Every collectible artwork—by virtue of its finite, material existence—is in constant danger of extinctions with time and erosion, and not infrequently by willful destruction. Can we imagine the terror of art lovers the world over if there were only one copy of "Romeo and Juliet" or of the "Fifth Symphony"? With extensions, we can all breathe easy, knowing that if one copy is destroyed there shall always be many more exactly like it. What better way of insuring our heritage for our posterity could there be? On the other hand, the true worth of every artwork will be judged not by high society and in an elite chamber but by history and generations. Or else, how would we ever know if the fame associated with the "Irises" is because of its price, or if the price is because of its merit as art? As it stands now, the painting is more famous for its price than its merit as a work of art, for the latter has never been tested in the true court of history's opinion. Only when there are unlimited identical copies—extensions—at a price reasonably affordable by anyone, can an artwork's true artistic value be judged. Or else, it cannot escape the critique of an elaborate hoax to keep the public in the dark and the art price in the sky.

Criticisms against forgery take two main forms, to now consider the oppositions to the idea: One, against the forger for his "low" moral character; and two, against the forgery for its lack of quality.

As for the first criticism, we have seen that the supposedly low moral caliber of the forger is not distinctly lower than that of the general public and certainly not much lower than many of the well known artists themselves. Of course, the implied meaning of criticism is in the forger's intention of profit-making with his forgery, masquerading as the original by the master. But, with the exception of Van Meegeren who had become a fairly wealthy man from the sale of his Vermeers, no one else made much money from forgery, and most died, like Dossena, in misery and obscurity. It has been the middlemen, sometimes unscrupulous fly-by-night types but more often respectable art dealers themselves, who have profited handsomely from their forgeries. For every major art scandal the trace has almost always led to a few famous art experts and reputable dealers as party to the scheme.

As for the second criticism, that forgeries lack the qualities of the original, it is technically incorrect and morally hypocritical. It is technically incorrect because such criticisms have almost always been made *after* the discovery, usually by the forger's own confession, not by the art establishment's own investigation. Besides, the fine critique by technical experts is useless because it does not lead to the discovery of yet-undiscovered forgeries by using the same criteria. It is morally hypocritical, on the other hand, because the art market is far from being the epitome of business ethics and aesthetic purity. It so happens that, even when some experts suspect forgery with incontrovertible evidence both aesthetic and scientific, as in the case of La Tour's "Fortune Teller" at the Met, art authorities have stoutly refused to listen or give credence to such suspicion. Obviously, where much money and high reputations are at stake, art's "realness" is entirely secondary to such higher concerns.

Extensions of masterworks, as outlined in the above hypothetical scenario, can meet both these criticisms and solve the problems that the criticisms raise. There will be no criticism directed at the person of the forger because he will not be accused of forging art for money or personal gains. Neither money nor personal gains in the form of fame, often notorious fame, can be available to tempt the extender. Nor would there be criticism directed against inferior quality because of the strict "quality control," in a manner of speaking, by the highest authorities now available in the art world. To assuage the fear about inferior quality, what would be the real difference between original masterpieces and extended masterpieces when both are declared indistinguishable by the testimony of experts? Our attitude toward the forgers should then properly be: WE WISH WE HAD MORE OF THEM!

Surely they embarrass the art establishment like a prominent sore and often shake it to its foundation with scandals. But that it is so has not been entirely the fault of the forgers or their forgeries. Rather, as we have seen in this book so far, it has been largely due to the very nature of collectible art itself in its various elements—namely, money, price, collection, and possession.

Extensions take money out of art and stand art on its own feet, now unhampered by the market mechanism which spawns the very proliferation of forgeries. It is not unlike the drug market: If demand cannot be met by legal supply, illegal supply will spring up to satisfy it. The market creates the hungry demand for art, yet it has only a handful with which to quench the hunger, and therefore at fabulous prices. Ironically, most artworks are created by humble, if not poor, artists; yet they become properties of the most exclusive social class. Forgeries have been called for, then, by this very market mechanism. Hence, extensions will resolve the demand-supply gap that now exists and compels the production of forgeries.

The association of art and money is rather unfortunate, as it is the most critical factor in the entire business of art in the Western world. It is unfortunate because art is one of the few human endeavors that are by their very definition thought to be unrelated to money. Aside from art, such non-pecuniary endeavors are traditionally found in devotion to religion, in pursuit of scientific (or philosophical) truth, and in the making of a revolution. Those who devote themselves to one of these endeavors consider their chosen mission a "calling," more as a missionary duty than as a profitable vocation. The calling takes priority over any other factors, both personal and public, and especially over money. Art as money-business distorts the very notion of art and destroys the very spirit which art claims to embody.

How does that process take place? What happens when art requires money and money becomes the precondition for art? Let's pursue this idea further.

Chapter 19

Fame and Fortune

One of the two main reasons as to why there is virtually no forgery in uncollectible art is simply that there is no money in it. Which is to say that there is no collection in uncollectible art, no one monopolizing everything related to the new (forged) work as it appears on the market.

When a collector bought a three-page manuscript of Beethoven containing a few measures of the "Ode to Joy" for $158,600 in 1988, he did not buy Beethoven's artwork and none of his art was locked up in the collector's private ownership. None of the "Ninth," in which the "Ode to Joy" is its last movement, would belong exclusively to the collector. A poem is being disputed anew as to whether it is by Shakespeare, a dispute going on since the nineteenth century. But the question has remained exclusively whether Shakespeare is indeed its author, not how much that would affect the price of the artwork. Those scholars who have disputed its authorship simply disagree on the ground of its quality, not any scientific examination or its signature. Those who support it as Shakespeare's refer to the "beauty" of the poem as being good enough to be Shakespeare's.

The other, perhaps equally important, reason to explain the paucity of uncollectible forgery is the *difficulty* which confronts the prospective forger. The technical and creative difficulty of forging a play purportedly by Shakespeare or a symphony by Beethoven, for example, would be so insurmountable that only those who possess equal or nearly equal talent to that of the masters themselves could contemplate such a task. And there are no such forgers in the world talented enough to do just that. (A fake Shakespeare was attempted in the late eighteenth century, which impressed Dr. Samuel Johnson's famed biographer Boswell as a real manuscript. Under critical examinations, however, the forger confessed to his mischief.) When a music organization offered ten thousand dollars in 1928 to anyone who could finish Schubert's "Unfinished Symphony" by completing its last two movements, no one could claim the prize in spite of its size.

In uncollectible art, quite unlike in collectible art, quality speaks for itself, regardless of the name attached to it. Not all Shakespeare plays are equally loved; not all Beethoven compositions are equally admired. Each play by Shakespeare and each composition by Beethoven, as famous as their creators, must fight for its recognition in the grinding process of historical judgment. It matters little if someone discovered a new (actually forged) manuscript by Shakespeare or a composition by Beethoven if its quality is not up to its author's accustomed place in art history, as we have seen in Mozart's newly-discovered symphony. Konstantin Bazarov tells of a Fritz Kreisler, a violin virtuoso of his time, as an example, who habitually used for his own compositions the names of composers well known and unknown. As a modest man, he simply didn't want to attribute so many compositions to himself. Although some critics were indignant when he confessed this in 1935, most others "Never thought it mattered very much, presumably because these would have been only marginal and minor works in the output of their alleged composers so that they wouldn't have made any really fundamental difference to it." It is perhaps this reason of quality, not name, that so many works in literature and music survive if they are good enough under "anonymous" authorships.

If the forger could indeed be good enough to produce a high quality Shakespeare or Beethoven, on the other hand, why would he bother to be a forger? He could be good enough to occupy a professorial chair at a prestigious university or conservatory! On the other hand, Keatings, Van Meegerens, or Wackers would never be given that sort of honor although their works were praised, albeit in someone else's name, on the highest level of accomplishment.

Just imagine, to enlarge our comparative understanding, two kinds of commissioned works for a large reward.

First, we want someone to come up with another Van Gogh, good enough to line up among the artist's own works. How many qualified Van Goghs would this contest produce? I would imagine too many to count. In collectible art real Van Gogh is not necessary to continue to produce more Van Goghs. Others can do that almost *just as well* as Van Gogh himself, and in some instances, even *better* than Van Gogh himself.

Second, we want someone to produce a sequel to "Romeo and Juliet" or a "Tenth" symphony by Beethoven. Which professor of English literature, which musical whiz kid, which artistic genius could indeed produce one that's good enough to satisfy experts and the public who know the quality of their works to which they are accustomed?

The point in this illustration is obvious. Only William Shakespeare can produce Shakespeares; and Ludwig van Beethoven Beethovens. Shakespeares and Beethovens can be imitated as a form of flattery, not faked or extended. Do we have too few Shakespeares and Beethovens, so that we need more of their works through extensions? No, we need not worry about the limited size of their respective output. For what they have produced can be reproduced in unlimited performances and copies the world over at relatively cheap prices. Anyone who wants to enjoy a Shakespeare play is able to do so almost at any time with practically no expense involved. Unlike Van Gogh's copies, Shakespeare's inexpensive performances or copies only increase the master's reputation.

We know why it is easy to extend or fake collectible art, for, regardless of what experts say about the "spirit of the age" which only the original is supposed to show, it is relatively easy to learn the technique of the masters and apply the technique to different subjects. Acquiring technique, even a difficult technique, is a matter of technical competence, an eye for fidelity, and repeated training. The extender or faker can use any subject, within the range of the master's own style, for all he has to do is repeat the same technique with different subjects. Each artwork thus produced will pass for an "original" work of art. For almost any master, his entire artworks within each stylistic period are remarkably alike and repeated. What is often called originality in collectible art is merely the stylistic stamp of the master, for example, the geometric figures of Picasso or the bright, bold color scheme of Van Gogh. A Vermeer needs not be totally different from another Vermeer and, indeed, it isn't. The extender or faker, once familiar with the stylistic personality, can continue to do this with relative ease. Besides, the forged artwork is generally hidden from public viewing, a fact which also favors the ease of forgery-production by protecting it from merciless examinations under critical eyes.

In uncollectible art, we also know why it is difficult to extend or fake. In it, the extender or faker has to create the whole range of ideas as well as master the technique. Mastering the stylistic idioms of a composer, which any reasonably trained person can do, for example, does not help the extender or faker, for it is only one-half of the job. In fact, it is less than that, for he must deal with the "ideas" as well, which only the original artist can conceive. It is known that Mozart's symphony can be produced by a computer which is programmed with the composer's musical idioms. But the computer-imitated Mozart merely *sounds* like Mozart, which can never *pass as* a Mozart.

The ease with which collectibles can be forged and accepted as real, and the difficulty with which the forgers of uncollectibles must contend in their forgery-production, hence the proliferation of the former and the paucity of the latter, can now be seen as contributing to the corruption in the marketplace.

In short, collectible art is chiefly associated with "fortune," and uncollectible art with "fame." Shakespeare and Beethoven are famous without creating fortunes with their work; Van Gogh and Picasso are famous primarily by being the source of fortunes. What corrupts art at the marketplace is fortune, not fame, or fortune as the precondition for fame. Thus, true art is established by fame; false art is created by fortune. Hence true art is possible only if fame and fortune are separated from each other. Fame and fortune, the two central concepts of art in Western civilization, therefore, can also enlighten us in our pursuit of truth in art.

First, we need to be clear about our terms.

"Fame" derives from a particular deed that is publicly, socially, and historically acclaimed as virtuous. The deed is a personal accomplishment for the famous person but the beneficiaries are always the public, the community, or humanity, not himself. Once acclaimed, fame is permanent and not generally transferable person to person. If the father is famous, his son does not normally inherit that fame. Artists derive fame for their artistic achievement; philosophers and scientists for their pursuit of truth; revolutionaries for their ideas of a new society; and saints and religious teachers for their profession of faith. Thus, fame is given only by history and public acclaim.

"Fortune" derives simply from the accumulation of wealth by an individual, which is a personal, self-centered, and private reward. It is primarily manifest in the simple possession of things, with their specific value in their own time and place, owned by one person but transferable to someone else. Fortune's stay in one person's possession is temporary and accidental, and, having no meaning to anyone else who doesn't share it, it only helps the person who owns it at the moment. Fortune is centrally dear to businessmen, mercenaries, merchants, workmen, prostitutes, and other varieties of vocations designed specifically for the pursuit of fortune on various levels. Thus, fortune can be taken by anyone who seizes it.

Historically, fame and fortune have been conceived as two separate and contradictory concepts. Fame and fortune were sought by two different types of people and through two different ways of attaining them. Fame was sought—if at all—by scholars, artists, statesmen, and revolutionaries. Their "pursuit" of fame took them on the high road to scholarship, art, statesmanship, and utopian ideals. A Southern scholar in the nineteenth century typically dedicated his diary to his "soul and to Fame," which, to him, meant virtuous deeds and great scholarship. Fortune, on the other hand, was sought by money-mongers and mercenaries who pursued it by offering their services to whomever would bid the highest. Fortune-seekers and -hunters made no pretenses, of course, at the niceties of virtue or immortality. Thus, fame and fortune were always kept apart as a social practice and as a moral precept.

It is only in market society in our modern times that the two notions have become conceived as two sides of the same coin, one entailing the other and one natural to the other. Not only are they considered compatible, creating neither a social conflict nor a moral dilemma in their compatibility, they are also regarded as prerequisite for each other. A famous person—a best-selling writer—expects to be famous for the very reason of his fortune. In our current society, where community and self maintain no clear distinction, for all is now considered in terms of "self," fame and fortune are thus understood as one continuous personal reward.

How do fame and fortune relate to our understanding of art?

Fortune, when linked to collectible art, corrupts it through the dominant workings of money, price, sales, and collection. An artwork's fame is strictly tied to its fortune. In fact, it is safe to say that a collectible artwork's fame *is* its fortune. Unlike in uncollectible art, a famous work in collectible art is also a famously expensive commodity. There is no way collectible art can avoid corruption by fortune. With each famous artwork, the artist, if still living, gets money for his art; the collector owns it, and no one else; the dealer makes a profit from the deal. But this fortune is also the creator of its fame as well. What used to be given only by history and only for great thoughts and virtuous acts can now be given to anything that costs a lot of money. Consider Van Gogh's "fame" that has steadily grown with the steady growth in the "fortune" of his artworks. While he was alive he couldn't give away his artworks. In 1890, not long after his death, his artworks sold for $20 a piece; by 1900, it rose to $200 a piece; by 1925, it commanded $15,000 a piece; by 1987, it skyrocketed to $50,000,000! Now, Van Gogh is the perhaps most "famous" painter in the world. When fortune and fame thus intersect in collectible art, only false art results from it. Fame brought on by fortune only glorifies the accumulation that results from the fortune, not the deed. Every artist now wants to be as famous—or as fortunate— as Van Gogh!

True fame cannot be claimed; it can only be given by history. Shakespeare and Beethoven are famous without their corresponding creation of fortune from their artworks. All uncollectible artists have acquired their fame without fortune, as all true artists must. Nor is their art considered a money-maker as in the more profitable sense of collectible art. In the uncollectible artist and in his art, fame and fortune stay almost strictly separated. Even in the best of times the uncollectible artist is no fortune-maker with his art. He pursues fame, if the term pursue is an appropriate one, not fortune. But his pursuit of fame is always *through* his artistic accomplishment, not through the price-jockeying or fortune-mongering of the marketplace. None of the uncollectible art forms in literature, drama, music, philosophy is a big money-maker; none of those who pursue these art forms expects to strike it rich with his art. Unless, of course, they want to make it big as best-selling writers, composers, whatever, in which case they are pursuing neither art nor fame, but their personal fortune, and thus cannot properly be called artists.

In collectible art, on the other hand, too much fortune is pursued by and is rewarded to the artist. The pursuit makes him a false artist, and the reward makes him a corrupt human being. Every artistic "break" either in style or in fame is instantly accompanied by its corresponding increase in fortune. Jasper John's "Diver" has sold for close to five million dollars, a record, while the artist is still living. By that reckoning Johns is the most famous living artist in America today. And also the richest. Every artist is a Jasper Johns at heart and every artwork looks at the "Diver" for inspiration. The dollar figure dances in every artist's eyes and the sound of an auctioneer's gavel beats in every artist's ears.

The collectible artist forsakes fame by pursuing fortune and lets fortune take care of his fame. "Successful artists," observes Benita Eisler in her book *Class Act* which could have easily been titled "How Artists Become Corrupt," describing what might be called a typical journey from fame to fortune, "are very sophisticated and adroit, adept at working with politicians and...'the economic and corporate forces' to achieve their own objectives....When artists become successful, they start associating with other 'communities.' You get invited to these people's houses. Soon you start feeling more and more comfortable. Your host and *his* peers are part of your world now, and if you're shrewd and sensitive and articulate, you start adapting. You start learning their language." As the artist feels comfortable in the new setting of the "economic and corporate forces," his corruption as an artist sets in and his art "adapts" primarily as a source of fortune-making.

There is no way of telling what is true art and what is false art unless we can apply one singular criterion: Money. Only when money is removed, and historical judgment rendered without its interference, can we tell if anything claiming to be true art is indeed true art. Thus, true art emerges inevitably as *famous art* without its accompanying fortune. "Romeo and Juliet" is true art because there is no fortune in its fame. The "Irises" is false art because we have no idea what its fame is; we only know about its fortune. Art's value is made clear and valid only when it is judged by fame, not fortune. Fame is historical and public; fortune overnight and private.

Not only is the art market itself a hoax, for it manufactures artworks that, by any standard of reality, do not exist, thus encouraging forgeries which are equally nonexistent. The art market by virtue of its role in fortune-creating and fortune-making also corrupts the very art form and those who may sincerely pursue the craft.

I have suggested extensions as a way out of this dilemma, which would break up the phantom art market by supplying more artworks than are currently sold and bought. By making art available to a wider audience—as the master artists would surely have approved—every artwork can now derive its art merit strictly from the public and the open forum of history. But the problem of collectible art does not stop here, at the corruption of the marketplace. It is much deeper than perhaps all of us may realize. It is the problem of collectible art itself, for we still don't know what it really is. We must have a better understanding of collectible art itself, both classic and modern, in order to better comprehend the comedy and insanity that characterize art and the art market.

What is *really* art? What is really *in* a picture? Is there really something in art that is so precious, so expensive, and so wonderful that is worth all that money and fame? Or, are we just being hoaxed into believing that there is *something* there indeed? The next few steps that we are about to take must necessarily be the most perilous and daring in our investigation that we have undertaken so far.

But we cannot stop here. We must go wherever our commonsense and logic take us, no matter how perilous or daring it may be. If we didn't, we would be about as hypocritical as the art establishment that we have been critically examining.

Chapter 20

The Naked Emperor

Art experts frequently write and lecture on this theory, that concept, and the other meaning in art. Most of the time, however, their discourses are incomprehensible as they are uninteresting. We on the outside looking in, even with fair intelligence, have no idea what they are talking about. Some of us, failing to comprehend them at all, rather sheepishly assume that there must be "something" there that is understood only by experts and politely defer to their authority in obscurity. But at this point of our journey, we can neither assume the validity of their professed knowledge, nor defer to their presumed authority in art. As we now know, their knowledge now seems woefully obscure and their authority wholly empty.

But is this necessarily their fault? Not quite. I believe, and this is the topic of our present consideration, that there is something inherently different about collectible art. As we have seen in its many instances, that something makes their knowledge impossible to be consistent and their authority impossible to be true. In many ways, it is not unlike the blind men with an elephant. It takes an outsider looking at the whole scene who can make any sense of their confused knowledge and empty authority. Great knowledge on an ambiguous subject cannot be clear; great authority on an empty subject cannot be real.

What's in a picture? We ended the last chapter with this question, and we must deal with the question here in order to solve the problems of expert knowledge and authority. What indeed is in a picture?

We have described collectible art as "easy art," easy in the sense of being easy to "complete" a work, easy to "become" an artist, and easy to be "original" with the work. But this ease in creative labor must demand its price in the very properties of art. What's easy art? What kind of ramifications or implications does this "easy art" have in its own self-presentation as art? Art lovers the world over are told to be "serious" with their approach to art; to experience a "profound" impact from art; and to appreciate the "titanic," "Olympian" struggle that the artist has waged to "create" his work for the world in our behalf. But how does this *easy* art square with the *serious, profound, titanic, Olympian* exhortations of art?

If Picasso could produce a picture between the two puffs of his cigar as de Hory commented (the accuracy of this statement is irrelevant), what are we to find in it that is serious, profound, etc., etc? There comes a time, like right now, when an artist or his art form must pay the price for the ease with which it is presented as art. The artwork created between the two puffs of a cigar can only be approached between the two puffs of the viewer's own cigar. The importance of the artwork can be compressed equally well in that time period. As the saying goes, what comes easy goes easy as well. It is asking too much on the part of the artist or his art form to be taken seriously when they themselves are not serious. Of course, not all collectible art can be executed in such a short time span and with such consummate ease—just consider Michelangelo's Sistine Chapel—, but the point is still the same.

The shortcomings of collectible art, notably painting, as "easy art," are inevitable in all aspects of its existence: The *artist*, the art *form*, and the *effect*. Let's consider each of these issues:

First, the artist. Being a collectible artist requires a remarkably little *sustained discipline* for his creativity. I know anyone who says this would be considered slightly mad. But it must be said: The kind of creative energy that an average collectible artist puts out of himself and into his work is *not that much*. The total conception and execution of a painting—especially a modern painting—is equivalent to a paragraph in literature, a small tune in music, a passing footnote in philosophy, and often even less than that. It is possible that the conception can take much longer than execution perhaps in modern art, or the other way around perhaps in classic art. But the end result is still the same. His thoughts can be as incomplete, as incoherent, or as juvenile as his painting, but, with the right circumstances and fortuitous expert opinions, can be hailed as great art. Virtually anyone can be a "great" artist if he has paint, canvas, and brush—and, of course, good luck with galleries and critics. To be an average artist, on the other hand, one only needs the former.

Second, the art form. The shortcomings of the art form itself—a one-dimensional, frozen-moment representation of thought or reality— are much more serious. Even with the best of intentions and creative abilities, there is only so much an artist can say through this medium. (One might say the same thing about film, which is a series of "many pictures" strung together. But film is not a series of pictures, it is a *story* put in visual form that can stand on its own without the pictures, so to speak.) In other words, even in the best of circumstances art says very little either by saying the obvious—in Biblical themes, portraits, illustrations—, or by confusing the saying—in modern art. In the worst circumstances, it says nothing as in the empty canvas or says something through none of the art's own effort as in the shovel. In a sense, it is so easy to "trivialize" the art form into meaninglessness and insignificance even with the best of intentions.

Suppose Shakespeare wrote an insignificant poem, Beethoven composed a poor piece, or Plato mused on bread-baking. Would it *survive* the mercilessly grinding machine of historical judgment only because their names would be on the work? Not likely. But compare that with any scratch paper, any doodling, any casual drawing of Michelangelo, or Van Gogh or Picasso. Undoubtedly, if presented in the art market today, the latter would be collected as high art and at high prices. Art collectors as a rule pay a considerable amount to buy any practice drawings that the masters left behind, as if they *were* art. As collections, they are significant. As art, they are trivial. But in reality, collection *and* art are one and the same.

Of all art forms, it is only in collectible art that art and trivia merge so comfortably and effortlessly. A collector who buys Van Gogh's scratch papers would also buy Napoleon's toilet articles, Gandhi's loincloth, or a queen's underwear as long as they are available and expensive. Thus, collection or collectibility itself trivializes what is being collected, which is about as trivial as collecting the signatures of celebrities. Van Meegeren confessed in court that forging a Rembrandt or the "Emmaus" was "relatively simple," but forging the signature, the most meaningless and trivial part of all art, was "the hardest job." Unless we speak of trivia, in which case the origin of the toilet article (Napoleon), of the loincloth (Gandhi), or of the underwear (the queen) is all that is important, why would we think of the authorship or the origin more important than anything else?

It is in this sense that the collectible art form suffers its gravest shortcoming. *Anyone* with brush, paint, and canvas can *claim* to have created art and *expect* it to be TREATED AS ART, HOWEVER TRIVIAL, INSIGNIFICANT, OR INCOMPLETE. It would be tantamount to expecting one's daily diary, "personals," or silly written thoughts to be treated as literature; or any tune that comes to one's mind as artistic music; or any private musings of no consequence as profound philosophy. But in collectible art, and notably in painting, any scratch, any doodling, any brush stroke, or any drawing *insists* upon being thought of as art as long as it can be framed or mounted. Only in collectible art can a work that has absolutely no disciplined creativity in a more or less completed form can claim the status of art. It can be *anything*, or it can be *nothing*, as long as it is *something*, as long as it can be framed or mounted, displayed, and sold. A person who is baffled by it all only shows his ignorance; one who protests that it makes no sense is an art-hater; anyone who questions the legitimacy of such an exercise doesn't understand that there are many theories, concepts, and approaches in art.

Is there anything *really* to collectible art under these circumstances? We must raise the question again and again. What would happen if a museum framed and displayed a five-dollar "nonsense" artwork as if it were a great work of art? Would anyone notice the difference? The public would continue to be baffled by it but wouldn't dare raise any questions about it, attributing this bafflement primarily to their art ignorance. Just as surely as this public response, there will be many art critics and experts who would lavish their praise on it, as they have done so many times on forgeries. What would happen, on the other hand, if the New York Philharmonic Orchestra performed a five-dollar "nonsense" music for its audience, or if a soprano sang like a baritone in an opera? As predictably as anything, there would be a howl of laughter and protest. Any critic or expert who expounds on it as "great" music would be laughed off his job. But why is such an event unlikely in collectible art, notably in painting?

Nelson Goodman, Konstantin Barazov, and others have observed that music is both "unfakable" and unfaked. Goodman's reason is that copies and the original are identical, while Barazov's is that there is no "market" for forgeries in music. Both observations are correct as an explanation for the paucity or, rather, impossibility of forgeries in music—and to a similar extent in literature and philosophy. We will just add our third explanation that has already been introduced: Uncollectible art in general is *too difficult* to forge, well beyond the range of any prospective forger contemplating a Shakespeare, Beethoven, or Plato forgery, as we have already seen earlier. It is mostly unthinkable that a forger, even a talented one, could create a whole play to pass for a Shakespeare, a whole symphony for a Beethoven, a whole dialogue for a Plato.

But this simple fact sends us right back to the inevitable point of *ease* with which collectible art can be forged, that we must grapple with and possibly to understand. The only conclusion we can logically draw from all the known facts is simply that: There is nothing in collectible art that is so difficult to copy or forge. As there is nothing real in it, there is nothing too difficult to copy or forge. Consider the worst-case possibility: Who couldn't bring in another empty canvas or another Black-and-Decker shovel as an artwork, that is so different from Jo Baer's own or Duchamp's Black-and-Decker? Or, consider the best-case possibility: Even the greatest artist like Michelangelo or Van Gogh can be copied and forged with relative ease by any talented forger, as happened too many times to count. When each of these originals cost in the millions, why would they—indeed, why *should* they—*not* be copied and forged?

Third, the effect. Right off, what artistic effect shall we expect from something that anything can become and can be produced by anyone who wants to claim the honorific title of artist? The answer: Nothing much. Anyone can say anything about anything as a great work of art and make a career out of saying it. But we cannot accept that as serious art stuff. They can glorify an elegantly-dressed Renaissance lady, an empty canvas, or triangles and rectangles in any way their ingenuity and enthusiasm would allow. But our commonsense and logic dictate that we should be more careful with their extravagant praise. In responding to Clive Bell's praise of collectible art that it "carries a person...out of life and into ecstasy" and "transforms us from the world of man's activity to a world of aesthetic exaltation," Professor Mark Sagoff dryly commented that the critics "speak of art in the same breathless terms that users of drugs sometimes speak about marijuana or cocaine."

Edward Hicks, the nineteenth century American painter, described painting as "one of the those trifling, insignificant arts which has never been of substantial advantage to man." For what reasons are we to agree with him, a substantial painter himself? Let's take the most famous painting in history, the "Mona Lisa" by Leonardo. What can we say about it? That it is in the Louvre, Paris, or that its insurance estimates its value at 200 million dollars, or that its "inscrutable expression of unfathomable emotion," as a writer puts it, made the painting famous. Of the three things that made it famous, the last is the only artistic reason for its fame. Most of us will never visit Paris to have a fleeting glimpse of a famous painting and be able to tell our friends that we have seen the painting. The insurance estimate of 200 million dollars or so makes no practical sense to outsiders like us, outsiders both in finance and in collection. But what can we say about the inscrutable expression of unfathomable emotion? What indeed? I will venture to say this: Any modern actress in the caliber of Meryl Streep can manage the inscrutable expression of unfathomable emotion much more convincingly and with greater depth, and is available to viewing for a few dollars in one's own living room than "Mona Lisa" herself. What does the inscrutable expression of unfathomable emotion in a painting that is thousands of miles away in some museum that one will almost certainly never see *do* for one as a work of art?

If the "Mona Lisa" were destroyed (threatened many times) or stolen (happening once) or sold (an unlikely event), the rest of the world would know about it and would talk about it some primarily because such an event would be on television. But what else would it do? If the "Mona Lisa" were as great an artwork as it is claimed to be, why don't we see its copies in the quantity everywhere that we see in Shakespeare's or Beethoven's or Plato's works? What is the *real* connection—artistic, cultural, emotional, whatever—that I feel with the "Mona Lisa"? On my part, the only honest answer I can give is, Nothing. Zero. Zilch. It is the most famous painting in history, yet it doesn't *do* anything for me as a work of art and is famous for reasons that have nothing to do with art. The "Mona Lisa" can exist forever in the Louvre, but as far I—and many others like me—am concerned, IT MIGHT AS WELL NEVER HAVE EXISTED. What difference could its nonexistence possibly make for me or for anyone else? Even for those who profess to love it, they can't get into "ecstasy" or "exaltation" just looking at its copies.

To lesser extents because they are lesser works, this is true of all other paintings or sculptures. Something so precious, so beautiful, so wonderful that exists in some faraway land one never gets to see is about the stupidest thing one can get all excited about. Watching a local sunset would be a much more practical and more satisfying experience. A collector might be excited about the prospect of *owning* the painting as part of his collections, but that excitement has nothing to do with art. It has to do with *collecting* it. So, that's a lot of ado about nothing. A critic described Vermeers—presumably the real Vermeers—as revealing the "calmness of heart," and the "nobility of heart." But the same thing we said about the "Mona Lisa" could also be said about Vermeers: If one is seeking the calmness or nobility of heart, one can find it in any local park, or in looking at a tree, a deer, or a goldfish. I doubt very much, on the other hand, if such calmness and nobility of heart would cost millions, whether the viewer's own heart would be so calm or noble at the price.

As is obvious, what the experts get all excited about is really nothing but the *price*, or the *market value*, or the *ownership*, not art itself. For, as art, these great works do absolutely nothing for anyone. But as market commodities costing millions, not unlike glamorous people, they are enough to turn anyone's head. Somehow these two totally irreconcilable elements—money and art—are fused in the critic's mind and confuse him as "artistic value." As we now know, the true artistic value of these artworks has never been established apart from their market value. And their true artistic value we would never know, as long as market prices describe their supposed importance in the art world, not their actual appreciation historically and publicly expressed.

On the other hand, how long can an ordinary, intelligent, sympathetic person look at an artwork without being bored by what he is looking at? The human senses—of which the eye is the primary one—have the tendency to get bored with the same subject, no matter how exciting, beautiful or wonderful initially. It is in the very nature of the senses. How long can one eat the same food everyday, although it was the greatest food he always wanted, and enjoy it every time? How many people can still repeat, after ten years of marriage, the same excitement of the first time they made love? If we stood in front of the "Mona Lisa" or the "Irises," to fully appreciate its artistic value even if such a long viewing was possible, how long can we stand looking at it without being bored by it? Now, of course, there are people who confess to be deeply moved by an artwork, experiencing all sorts of psychidelic emotions, but I suspect that these people will be just as deeply moved by a lot of other things. Also, what if the artwork that moved them so deeply turned out to be a forgery?

Some art-people I know tell me that there is no *one* interpretation for any artwork. Different people, they say, should draw "their own conclusions" from viewing the same work. Although this is said in defense of art's ability to evoke various responses, it reveals another element of emptiness in collectible art. We would ask, then, if this were the case, why bother to create these so-called artworks in the first place, if the emotion they evoke in the viewer is determined entirely by the *viewer* himself, not by the *artwork* itself? Why not frame a newspaper clipping or mount a piece of animal dung—which I suspect has already been done by some modern artists—or, still better, frame or mount a nothing, and let people draw their own conclusions about what the object could possibly mean? So, the "Mona Lisa's" expression is *inscrutable* and its emotion *unfathomable*, is that what makes it the most famous and possibly the greatest work of art, when what it says is totally unclear? In my opinion as an outsider, the "Mona Lisa" is perhaps the biggest nothing—what else can "inscrutable" and "unfathomable" mean? — that has beguiled everyone in history.

That paintings, even famous ones, mean very little to us in their emotional, artistic impact, if we are inclined neither to comedy nor insanity over art, is precisely the reason why they hang in public places such as shopping malls, restaurants, offices, and homes. THEY DO NOTHING AND NOBODY NOTICES THEM. (Imagine, for contrast, hanging a sign that says "Support Communism!" at an American mall, or "Free Enterprise!" at a Moscow square.) Of course, this does not mean they have no functions at all, for they do. As illustrations of great events, like the Biblical events, or great personalities, like the portraits of the famous and powerful, they do serve a definite historical, educational function. But how these functions are related to art is unclear. We shall look at this issue again in the next chapter.

Finally, the *graphic* represents a generally lower form of expression on the scale of human communication than the *literary*. Pictures convey messages much more quickly and simply than words, it is true, but such messages must be of a lower origin, such as "danger," "men's" and "women's" restrooms, street signs of "stop," "no turn," "airport," and so on. Children can start drawing much sooner than they can create their own ideas with words. Even chimpanzees can speak picture-language. That's why quick signs make the meaning much clearer and more to the point than literary descriptions.

As a graphic form of expression, collectible art can achieve only a limited objective in its range of communication: To create primarily a "sensory," "psychological," and "momentary" reaction, rather than an intellectual reflection, from the viewer; to convey an artistic idea that is wholly incomplete in its formulation, only superficially-involving in its emotional communion, and widely subjective in its interpretations; and to suggest the artist's inner self that is only partially crystallized and developed, and largely unsatisfactory and unexplained as human experience.

After all this has been said, then, we might dare venture to raise some rather radical questions: Should collectible art, in light of such shortcomings inherent in its artist, its form, and its effect, and flaws that are historical facts—over one-half of all artworks in circulation being forgeries—be called "art" at all? Shouldn't it be separated from "truer" art, namely, uncollectible art, and simply be called a "COLLECTIBLE" with the same degree of significance as collecting famous toilet articles, loincloth, or underwear?

It is all very wonderful that we have such and such a treasure in such and such a place and it costs such and such an amount of money, and it is called "art." But, so what? It is no art to me, it does nothing for me, I cannot enjoy its copies without being made a fool, I will perhaps never see it in my life time, and it is not doing any good to anyone or for anyone except that one collector in his pathological obsession or that one museum in a faraway place. Celebrate it all you want, but the art-emperor is naked and only the stupidest among us would fail to notice it.

So, I still ask: In what ways and, more importantly, *why* should we, ordinary people everywhere, join in the celebration of the glitz, the hype, and the hoax that seem to excite only the obsessed, the befuddled, and the idle rich—all in the name of art?

I concede that what has been said above is indeed a mouthful, and we need to chew on it slightly longer until it has become more palatable and digestible. Let's, to help with our digestion and palate, therefore look at the the classic masterworks and modern art separately in the light of what has been said.

Chapter 21

Craft or Art?

Most art books trace the "history" of art through the entire scope of human development, generally agreeing with the classification of "classic" art and "modern" art, using the nineteenth century as the transitional period. Leonardo, Michelangelo, and Raphael, among others, are said to be artists of the classic period. Picasso, Chagall, and Warhol, among others, covering the divergent styles from Post-Impressionism to Pop-Art and all the variations between them, may be roughly grouped as artists of the modern period. Van Gogh, Cezanne, and Renoir, among others, can be said to represent the transitional period from classic to modern.

Although most art writers speak of classic and modern as two styles of art in *continuity*, there is no resemblance between the two, other than the most superficial of elements, namely, that both use canvas, paint, and brush to draw and that both types of works are sold and collected as art. In terms of the actual subject-matter, of the underlying philosophy, and of the purpose and function of their activity, they stand poles apart from each other. They have virtually nothing in common.

In science, modern science is built upon the old; in the humanities, Plato is still the dominant figure in the Western mind; in social thought, the main stream ideas are centuries old. In collectible art, literature and music are still practiced with the masterworks of old as their models. In collectible art, however, a Renaissance artist and a modern artist seem to have practically nothing in common. In fact, they are in many ways diametrically opposed to each other, which gives us on the outside a better glimpse of their true nature.

First, a few words on classic art.

It is fairly clear even from an outsider's cursory view that what is called classic art is based on some "external" principle of aesthetic value. The artwork is to reflect the best possible conformity to some external criteria for accuracy, beauty, and perfection. Anatomical and historical accuracy is deemed important, and often accuracy and beauty are considered synonymous in classic art. Its main purpose is functional, decorative, and official record-keeping, according to the prevailing social requirements, be they for the Church or well-to-do households. Guided almost wholly by the external criteria and purpose, the classic artist rarely looks "internally" within himself. Although the personality of a Leonardo or of a Michelangelo towers over the works, it is still the *work* that stands out; the artist's personality, psychic makeup, and internal musings are well kept under the requirements of technical perfection, balance, and elegance in the work. In short, classic artworks can be said to resemble "artistic photographs," or, in the parlance of music, "program art"—as opposed to "pure art" of modern times—that is conceived, commissioned, and produced for a specific purpose or program in mind. With the decline of religion in largely secular Western civilization, and, more importantly perhaps, with the introduction of photography, however, classic art both in its subject-matter and purpose, as well as technique, has become obsolete.

What, then, is the renown "art-ness" in classic artworks? Why are they regarded as great works of art? Where classic art is concerned, the art market defines technical perfection and aesthetic beauty as the supreme criteria. Art experts, in assessing classic artworks, almost never ask about the "meaning," the "metaphor," or the "message" of this or that artwork. The questions they raise are most often the questions of external authenticity: How perfect and beautiful is it? During the two-Leonardo trial—re the "La Belle Ferronniere" affair—, for example, the entire testimony of experts was devoted to the anatomical details of supposed perfection in one version as opposed to the supposed imperfection in the other. (The controversy would never have arisen if both had been photographs, for anatomical details and accuracy were virtually all that the experts were arguing over. Modern photographers and models could create the most perfect realism any time, superior to classic artworks in every way.) Hence, technical fidelity to reality and superiority in its rendition, a fairly negligible talent in today's photographic copying ability, are considered the hallmark of greatness in classic art. Thus, technical perfection, fidelity to realism, and elegant beauty are the most significant elements in it.

Being conceived, commissioned, and produced for specific functional purposes—either official or familial—classic art in that sense is perhaps much more technical-historical record-keeping than art. Which is to say, all those requirements could have been fulfilled much better with our modern techniques of realistic copy-making and illustrating. Modern anatomical charts demonstrate greater accuracy than Leonardo could have ever imagined possible. The elegantly dressed Renaissance ladies and gentlemen, on the other hand, have little emotional appeal to our modern taste. The religious subject and mood which dominate classic art also suffer a similar fate in our radically secular civilization. In short, classic art is but a demonstration of first-rate craftsmanship and, if anything, of a second-rate art for the reasons that we shall consider below.

Then, what makes the classic artworks so precious, so wonderful, and so expensive? The answer that readily comes to mind is their *rarity*. There are so few recognized artists of the classic period, and so few of their works are reputedly in existence that each one of them becomes something of a rare presence. Corollary to the first, of course, is their suitability for the purpose of exclusive collection. That there are so few in existence is just right for the very idea of collection for high society. Or else, collecting classic artworks would have been as commonplace as collecting stamps, coins, or rocks.

But this does not answer our question, for the fact of rarity and the fact of art-ness have nothing to do with each other, in the same way collection and art are wholly unrelated. What is rare is not necessarily good art, for we collect precious gems without considering them art. Nor is good art necessarily rare, for copies and performances are abundantly available in all uncollectible art. Nor does everything that is rare become the subject of collection, for there are rare birds and plants that most people don't care to collect. Add to these also the fact that the condition of rarity is an artificially maintained one by the art market in the face of numerous forgeries circulating among the supposedly "rare" classic artworks. Rarity is also a serious defect, perhaps more importantly, yet in another sense: The rarity in classic artwork is its own worst enemy because of its unavailability to the rest of the world. Let's admit it. For something wonderful to do its wonderful work, it must *affect* as many people as possible—say, generations—and as inexpensively as possible for all humanity. Classic artworks of rarity may be rare enough to whet the wealthy collector's appetite, but have little or nothing to do with anything that is important enough for ordinary people like ourselves.

The idea of classic art as beautiful, a point most commonly referred to by art experts, also gets its twist in the presence of forgeries. All classic artworks are said to contain extraordinary beauty, but so are all the forgeries that pass as genuine. The beauty evoked in classic art is largely due to its technical superiority in craftsmanship. But this craftsmanship can be mastered easily, as has been in many instances, by modern forgers. If the classic masters were first-class craftsmen—with second-class artistic freedom and creativity because of their social and cultural restrictions as well as those of the medium itself—, the task for our modern forgers is made obviously that much easier.

Considering beauty as a condition for classic art, it is reasonable to say that what is beautiful is not necessarily art—as in sunsets, clouds, flowers, people—, nor is art necessarily beautiful as we see in many of the "great" works in uncollectible art. As noted above, the modern techniques of copying and illustration, with the aid of photography, can create far more aesthetically appealing graphic beauty than can be appreciated in classic art. Thus, neither rarity nor beauty in itself has anything to do with the enormous value we attach to classic art.

An alternative theory may be that the artworks reflect the "spirit of the age" and the creative impulse unique to the original artist. This is indeed a noble sentiment most often expressed by art experts and historians when they refer to classic art. This sort of sentiment—although so vague and unclear as to be meaningless—does have the ring of noble and civilized taste. But, other than representing those nice but vague sentiments and civilized tastes, this alternative explanation fails to satisfy those who want more precision and reason in their thinking.

It would be nice to share with the lovers of classic art those wonderful thoughts and feelings, but how are we supposed to be able to do just that? Consider the location and availability of those splendid artworks that are denied to all but the most exclusively wealthy and fortunate. There is only one precious copy hidden somewhere in a private vault or under guard at a remote museum. How is an ordinary person, neither rich nor living next to a museum where there are only few pieces available, supposed to share this noble sentiment embodied in the spirit of the age and the creative impulse? Art teachers and experts bubble over the slides they take during their obligatory tour of faraway museums and exhibitions. But why are their precious slides worth more than someone's holiday snapshots? What can we glean from the flickers on the screen in an art class, or from a glimpse or two of copies of rare masterworks in a handsome art illustration like some precious thing only the wealthy and fortunate few get to collect and enjoy? We admire artists like Leonardo, Michelangelo, and Raphael, not necessarily because of their artistic persuasion, but because, as civilized beings, we are *supposed* to admire them and their works. Yet, most of us have never seen any *real* work by any of them. We *know* that they are famous artists but are uncertain exactly *what* makes them famous artists.

The last point is really the crucial one. *What* have the classic masters *done* for my artistic growth? What am I supposed to have *learned* from their great artworks? It is all very wonderful that Michelangelo painted all those scenes on the ceiling of the Sistine Chapel, and the world admires him for that. But, alas, I have never been to that fabled Chapel, nor do I expect to be there any time soon. Suppose I *did* go there and looked at the frescoes? What would be the lesson of life that I would learn from them that we are supposed to get from such great works of art? Surely, they are rare and beautiful in all their facial expressions and anatomical details and proportions, etc., as everyone says. But what else?

Perhaps that no collector is wealthy enough to collect all the frescoes even if they were available for private collection?

Anatomical accuracy and perfection in form are the much admired qualities in classic art. But not only has this accuracy and perfection been surpassed by the later advancement in the techniques of perfect reproduction. It has also been made irrelevant by the changes in aesthetic standards. Leonardo may have been valued for his anatomical fidelity, as was emphasized much by the experts in the "La Belle Ferronniere" trial, but artworks are also praised precisely for the opposite reason of anatomical "inaccuracy" and "distortion." Samuel Palmer's so-called Shoreham period, for which there is "an insufficient supply" of works—somewhat alleviated by Tom Keating's own Palmers—is praised precisely for the forms that are, in Norman's words, "magically distorted and details exaggerated" and for their "idiosyncrasy." If technical perfection and fidelity to realism are the hallmarks of classic art, in fact, the very reason for its art-ness, then their opposite in imperfection and distortion can be just as much art.

In this sense, Sir Joseph Duveen, the self-assured expert who testified against the Kansas City version of "La Belle Ferronniere" by pointing out all the defects in its anatomical details, could have just as easily used such defects as artistic *compliments*. Or, Hope B. Werness's criticisms of Jesus in Van Meergeren's forgery of Vermeer as "insipid and sweet, sometimes miserably forsaken, always weak and powerless" could have just as easily been given as *praise* of the Jesus figure. Which leaves us in a dilemma once again.

It turns out that the reputed value of classic art is two-fold: Rarity and beauty. But, as we have seen, value in rarity is really the value that would please only collectors and market speculators, whereas value in beauty has nothing to do with art, for beauty in itself has no connection with art; it is also a quality that can easily be surpassed. That it is a thing of rare beauty may have its value in the scheme of things in this world, much vaunted and valued to be sure, but none of it has anything to do with what we would call artistic value.

So, why does classic art fall short of true art at all? The main trouble in its claim to art-ness is that it has little or nothing to say as its artistic statement. There may be people, like collectors and experts, who are satisfied with things of rare beauty as works of art. But many others, myself included, would look for something other than rarity and beauty in what is claimed and treasured to be a work of art. Besides, it is not necessary for rare beauty to have come from the hands of an artist, for it can be fashioned by chance and nature—like gems, sunsets—that have nothing to do with art or artist. But, taking art seriously, not frivolously or in obsession, we would still demand that the artwork, or the artist through his artwork, *say something* that expresses an artistic intention, purpose, or philosophy. But we find no such statements in classic artworks, as valuable and as heralded as they may be in other ways. (Actor Charlton Heston, who played Michelangelo in the film "The Agony and the Ecstasy," marvelled at the enormity of the artist's *labor* for the frescoes in the Sistine Chapel. But, of course, he should have also considered the enormity of labor required in the Great Pyramid or in the Great Wall or in the Panama Canal. The simple truth is that no one ever *collects* these enormous human creations and thinks them precious.)

Classic art—lacking a definite artistic statement in its rarity or beauty, other than the vaguely expressed sentiment of the "spirit of the age"— remains largely a meaningless rarity and a vacuous beauty. Its chief value lies in its great price for prestigious collection, hardly a significant factor in true art that must be universally available and enjoyable. Besides, to better comprehend the Spirit of the Age, we normally read history books and tour historical sites. Classic artworks are too unavailable and too incomplete for such a purpose.

So, what's in classic art? A lot of money for the collector's frenzy, a cause of obsessive envy and status claim—but little else.

Modern art's problems, as we shall see, are exactly the opposite of classic art's.

Chapter 22

The Best Art is Least Art

Unlike classic art, as we have just considered, modern art looks to itself, its "internal" psyche and purpose. Its main concern is no longer in representing or confirming external reality as closely and beautifully as possible. It is the artist himself, asserting his will and thought through his artworks, that now occupies center stage. With the decline of the functional, official, and historical reasons for art, the artist had to find a new purpose for its existence. Accurate renditions of reality and their technical perfection no longer being the aim of art in the technologically advancing world, the artist gradually turned to his "message," his "idea," and his whole being as the substance and subject of his art. The objective beauty in anatomical and external accuracy and superior craftsmanship gave way to the urgent need of the artist to express himself and his subjective reading of reality.

The medium itself became a forum for expressing his inner feelings, his existential thoughts, and his artistic philosophies. In this, modern art boldly declared its total independence from classic art as well as from its external reality as measures of beauty, excellence, and perfection. As the artist asserted himself more and more, however, his *art* itself has become less and less significant as a factor. Unlike the classic artist who let his artwork speak for itself, now the modern artist finds it increasingly necessary to supply his message, his idea, and his philosophy in non-artistic terms, essentially outside the medium itself. Picture has given way to thought, and objective fidelity to subjective assertion. Modern art has ultimately become what Tom Wolfe calls the "painted word." It is with these very ideas and words that modern art must live and die.

In many ways, the modern artist has freed himself from the very art medium itself which, in previous times, bound his whole being as an artist and his whole range of technical requirements as a craftsman. Now freed from his art and its technique, the artist has become a *true* artist in the sense that he is now in full control of his medium as well as his thought. His art need not be pictorial, in the traditional sense of the term, at all; his art need not be "art" at all, as long as the artist himself is honestly and sincerely represented in the new form of expression. If it is to be an empty canvas or a Black-and-Decker shovel, so be it, the artist has declared it to be the true representation of his thought and existence. If he is moody, ambiguous, and capricious in his self and his art, it is because such represents his reality accurately. Art is a process of self-revelation, not external duplication.

The self-image of the modern artist is that of a philosopher first, and a painter or a sculptor next, if at all; a human being first, a craftsman next, if at all. His task is no less than a total revelation of his inner self, his vision, his torment, his sentiment, his longings and sorrows, not the beautiful or perfect rendering of reality. He seeks purpose, not fidelity; he craves humanity, not technical perfection; he wants self-satisfaction, not a fulfillment of some official function. And nothing binds him in his quest for artistic honesty and personal integrity. The only force that regulates and guides him is his own inner self and its moral precepts. There is no official control, no technical standard, or no external conformity to follow. Thus, no longer bound by either technical convention or objective reality, the artist today is as free as he has ever been in history. In the parlance of music, once again, every artwork is now "pure" art; there is no "program" art which forces the artist against his artistic wishes or inner compulsions.

Such is the grand stage for modern art and the historical setting for its actors—the artists—to play out their roles in the world of art. How have they done with their artistic and historical roles? Not very well. As in so many cases in history, the freedom of modern art has become modern art's greatest enemy.

If the classic artist is a craftsman without philosophy, then, I believe, the modern artist is a philosopher without craftsmanship. If classic art is valued for its rarity, modern art is marketed through its *hype* and commercialism. If classic art is admired for its beauty and perfection, modern art is collected and displayed as expensive toys and fashionable gadgets. If classic art contains nothing of substance but external fidelity and predictable order, modern art is filled with messages, ideas, and philosophies that are largely incomplete, underdeveloped, and often incoherent. If classic art represents form without substance, modern art embodies neither the form nor the substance of any kind, degenerating often into a pictorial psycho-babble and self-indulgent but meaningless emotions. Every modern art form, by and large, is an experiment without plans, an assertion without philosophy, an artistic impulse without conformity to some public reality, and a forum for intellectual midgets trying to play the role of philosophical giants. Modern art's intention begins and ends on a psychiatrist's couch; its results are nothing clearer than ink-blots, and its achievement is a monumental silliness passing for profound ideas. The modern artist emerges as the most incompetent, neurotic, game-playing, corrupt, irrelevant, psycho-babbling, self-deluding, immature fantasist with all his art toys and all the walls at his disposal on which to throw his paint, whose idea of great art is on the level of a moronic prankster. His art is without shape, his art philosophy only half-molded.

Is this preliminary assessment too harsh for modern art? I think not. But for those who think I am unduly harsh on it, let's examine modern art further in its peculiar art form and the modern artist as the central figure in this nonsensical comedy of great insanity.

First modern art as an art form.

Modern art has much in common with modern social science. Both lack substance, not knowing exactly what they are supposed to be doing. Lacking in substance, yet existing within a structured environment—the artistic community and the university setting respectively—however, their enterprise tends to be increasingly superficial in contribution, their existence irrelevant as a technical community, and unsure of itself as a legitimate part of society. But this lack of substance does not discourage them from doing bold things, as if to justify their lack of substance with elaborate "methods" and often shocking sensationalism. Modern art and social science, similarly, are publicly noticed only when they do silly things that are of little value as substance. The artist might display a bizarre artwork, and the social scientist might announce an exotic scientific "discovery" to get a few laughs from the public and a few by-lines in the news media. Hence, both fields of endeavors tend to stress "theories" and "isms." All the "isms" in modern art—"Minimalism," "Structuralism," and so on—are matched only by those in social science. Both make up as many theories and isms as their ingenuity and desperation would allow, as if nothing is possible without them guiding their conduct. Finally, their similarities converge in their inconsequentiality in society, consisting mostly in silliness and emptiness. Neither modern art nor modern social science has much that is essential to society's well-being and happiness. They merely survive—and prosper in some individual cases—by their wits, smarts, and salesmanship.

Modern art is essentially a trivia that is marketed as art through the genius of hype. How else are we to take seriously all the fashions in modern art, subject to change as rapidly as the mood in the stock market. Consider all the forms of new art: "Abstract Art," "Pop-Art," "Minimal Art," "Concept Art," "AntiForm," "Micro-Emotive Art," "Impossible Art," "Possible Art," "Earth Art," etc., etc. as if modern art were a children's game. They tell me that there is much difference among these different "schools" and "theories" and "isms," one often chastising another as less art than itself, and so on, as Expressionism once denounced Pop-Art as non-art. But, aside from being modern art, they have one thing in common: They all take art as a game to play and to win. Their main weapon is psychological, not intellectual; their effect is sensory, immediate, and shallow, not thoughtful or reflective; their medium is graphic, relying more on shock-value than depth or meaning and confusing shocking with thought-provoking; their selling point is the transiency of human reaction like the latest fashion or cause, neither lasting, nor sincere in conception.

Most so-called modern artworks, without their price tags and collection implications, would only evoke either a mild bafflement or puzzled looks from the public. Or, sometimes and against their intended purposes, they are good for a few chuckles from the passersby. Neither rare in existence nor beautiful to look at, modern art is fairly non-sensical as human experience and nonexistent as a learning process. People looking at modern art rarely understand the artist's philosophy, nor do they leave it thinking that something has been learned, or at least felt in their hearts. Again, like social science, modern art is created for the amusement of those who seem to understand their doings as in-house jokes, but not for anyone else.

How is modern art conceived and produced? Let's assume the following, somewhat odd but not totally unrealistic scenario in the production of modern art:

1. A fairly well-known modern artist is planning to do an artwork, but interrupts his work and leaves his studio for a few minutes.

2. His ten-year old nephew visiting him, knowing nothing about art and thinking the canvas was a wash-cloth, sticks the bubble gum he has been chewing to the canvas. Being sticky, the gum has to be smeared all over the canvass in irregular shapes. The boy throws the canvas on the floor and leaves the studio.

3. A dog, a lab-chow mixed breed, comes into the studio through the crack in the door and, sniffing at the gum on the canvas, urinates on it, leaving a huge irregularly-shaped rings on the canvas. On the way out, the dog kicks a couple of cans of paint nearby, adding more figures and shapes to the canvas.

4. An art dealer friend of the artist's stops by on the way to his gallery and finds the canvas on the floor. At first puzzled by the strange mixture of shapes and colors, he gradually realizes the potential for the artwork as a significant breakthrough in "Random Art."

5. The dealer offers the just-returning and rightly puzzled artist a huge sum for the "artwork," which the artist of course accepts, by gladly signing the canvas and titling the work as "A Day at the Studio."

6. Now properly framed and displayed at the gallery, the artwork gets reviewed in the newspaper and becomes a pioneering landmark in "Random Art." Of course, on his next series of Random Art, the artist

adds a cat, a goat, a rabbit, and other assortments of possibilities to his art conception.

Unlikely? Yes, perhaps exactly in those steps and circumstances. But overall as a way of modern art production, hardly too unlikely or unusual. What passes for modern art does not go through a process, intellectual, artistic or otherwise, any more vigorous than the fortuitous steps described above. A story I heard from a local artist relates to a modern sculptor (by the name of Dorothy Gillespie, to insure the authenticity of the story) who sent her work to a museum in New York. Upon receiving her work, the museum wrote her, thanking her profusely for sending them her work of such and such shape and quality. The punchline is Dorothy Gillespie's reaction when she read their description of her sculpture: "My God!" she shrieked. "They haven't even unwrapped it yet!" But, was there *really* a difference between the real sculpture and its wrapping? I would like to know.

Modern art is one of the few things in society that require no particular qualifications to produce, if the above scenario sounds plausible enough. It is said that *anyone*, even a child, can be and *is* an artist. Nor does the sanity or the intellect of the artist matter that much. Modern art is so without criteria, external or otherwise, so wide-open as to be meaningless as a matter of structure, and so subjective-personal that any expression may be considered its proper domain. If experts see logic and coherence in the picture, they say its logic and coherence are its main features. If they see nothing but illogic and incoherence, they simply apply an appropriate art style to it, calling it a pioneering work in "Illogic-Incoherent Art." It can be orderly or chaotic, light or dark, large or small, a lot or very little on it, naturalistic or surreal, complex or simple, animal dung or broken glass, all it needs is a proper frame and display to qualify as art. In fact, an artist by the name of Piero Manzoni in his "Merde of the Artist," Merde meaning "shit" in French, actually used "fecal matters" in sealed packages as his artwork. (The artist died in in 1963 at the age of 30.)

Modern art also relies exclusively on the viewer's response for its existence, that is, how one *feels* about the artwork, no other criteria being relevant. Unlike other art forms, modern art as collectible art need not please everyone, just one critic, just one collector, just one dealer. We need not be elaborate in our defense of liking or disliking a particular artwork. If simple-minded, we can say we "like" the way it looks, feels, or just is. If sophisticated, we can describe our feelings in some fancy ways, such as, "I like the way harmony and disharmony are in harmony" (which is from a real art review in the Los Angeles *Times*) or "I like its oblique pragmatism—no flabby euphemisms here. There is a hopefulness in his thematic deconstruction" (which is from a Canadian movie). As anything or even nothing can pass as art, any response can also pass as an art response. Recall the Jackson Pollocks on exhibition in Australia, forgeries hung *upside down*, with no one, not even the expert who supervised the exhibition, being able to tell what was what and which side was the right side up. It is difficult to know really anything about modern art.

Speaking of anything and nothing being modern art, when I mentioned ink-blots earlier in reference to the nature of modern art, I wasn't joking. Showing two identical ink-blots on folded paper, the renown art historian H.W. Janson actually wrote in his imposing *The Picture History of Painting*, "With a bit of effort, it is not too difficult to find two galloping animals here." With a bit of effort, we can see anything in everything. We don't need something to see anything. Anything is something and anything is art. What is called "Conceptual Art," as described in Tom Wolfe's book, is really "Nothing Art," the artist doing as little art as possible or, often, no art at all.

How easy is it to forge modern art? According to experts and forgers, very easy. In fact, many believe that classic art is just too difficult to fake and takes too long to finish, whereas modern art forgery takes about as short a time as the actual time the original artist took, which can be anything from a few seconds to whatever. Forger Jean-Pierre Schecroun could do a Picasso "in three minutes," as Robert Wraight tells the story. By contrast, Van Meegeren took years of preparation for his first Vermeer. This obvious difference, and the increasing sophistication of scientific methods in detection, makes modern art the favored choice of most forgers in operation.

How can something which takes very little to produce—either in time or in creative effort—cost so much, the latest being a Jackson Pollock titled "Search," presumably a real one and framed with the right side up, for five million dollars? How can something that has neither clear shape nor coherent philosophy be called art? Well, these questions in turn explain the incessant desire in the modern art community to "explain" everything—artworks, theories, meanings, styles, and so on— telling us about this or that aspect of modern art as if modern art could not stand alone by itself as art. (Obviously, it can't.) In classic art, such explanations and theories were both unimportant and unnecessary, because its subject-matter was self-explanatory—mostly Biblical and functional—and its style dictated by the requirement of fidelity to realism. Where neither the subject-matter nor the style is any longer tenable as a historical process modern art finds itself constantly having to explain everything about its art-ness.

Why is something so incoherent, so shapeless, so nonexistent as modern art allowed to be collected in public museums and possessed by wealthy collectors? Hanging paintings upside down and not knowing about it—although nothing astonishing in modern art—would be equivalent to staging Shakespeare's plays or performing Beethoven's symphonies *backward* and not knowing about it, if this state of affairs can be imagined. Unlike responding to modern art, in responding to such uncollectible art, we must articulate in some reasonable, but not necessarily sophisticated, terms of art appreciation why we like this or that play, or this or that symphony. If a totally "incomprehensible" play, or symphony, or philosophy were to be presented to the public, there would be an instant registration of public protest and ridicule. Suppose a printer throws his types to the ceiling and sets the pages as the types fall and calls it a book; suppose a composer throws his musical notes in the same manner and calls it music; suppose a philosopher formulates his thoughts in a comatose and calls it his philosophy? On the other hand, suppose a modern painter threw all his paint in the air and let it fall on his canvas and framed it and sold it as art; suppose a sculptor did nothing to his block of stone or wood, mounted it and sold it as art...

But in modern art, nothing is ever so outrageous enough to rate public indignation, ever nonsensical enough to evoke public ridicule. The most comic and the most insane are deemed perfectly acceptable as legitimate in modern art, and perhaps *only* in modern art.

Why is this state of comedy and insanity in modern art? For further explanation, let's shift our attention to the artist himself.

Chapter 23

All in the Name of Art

What kind of men (and women) decide to become modern artists and why do they spend their whole life creating meaningless "nothings" in the name of art?

First of all, none of the common logic and sane reasons that society requires of all its members—from brick layers to scientists—for their action is required of the modern artist and his action. Anything he does in the name of art, however infantile or senseless, is forgiven. In fact, the modern artist is so alien to the notion of common logic and sane reason that we habitually exclude them from our everyday human discourse in the same way we habitually exclude the astrologer, the psychopathic, and the moronic from the same expectations. We simply assume they are crazy. Thus, freed from the technical obligation of realism so that his pictures don't have to resemble *anything* in particular, and blessed with the "ease" of his craft so that he doesn't have to demonstrate his skill as a craftsman, he is as free as a child and as oblivious as a lunatic.

The modern artist, then, is suddenly without a function. He produces neither pretty pictures to look at, nor profound philosophy to reflect on. What he does reveal in his works is the largely incomplete and neurotic self-absorption of his inner mind that is neither here nor there. What he does produce as a result is the pictorial rendition of a remarkably immature, confused, and shallow personality in the artist. If he is a Minimalist—one who does his very minimum—, he is likely to think and work minimally but expect the public to give him the maximalist benefit of the doubt for his art, and hopefully at the maximalist price. So little is the modern artist involved with his art, intellectually as well as physically, that the artist could do a "modern art" picture in his sleep, in a drunken stupor, in a drug-induced comatose, with his eyes closed, or by letting his dog do it for him. Some enterprising modern artists like Mark Kostaby, as he appeared on "West 57th" in March 1988, hire others to do the work for him.

At best, the modern artist may have a chaotic mess of moods, reactions, and images, to judge him by what he produces, but no clear ideas. But this is the *essence* of modern art. It must be chaotic and meaningless to be thought of as art. If the artist's ideas were clear and well-articulated, he *could not* possibly produce what he in fact does. How could a person of clear and well-articulated ideas *not* produce an object either in pictures or words that is both clear and straightforward to the viewer or the reader? Clarity of ideas would make modern art simply impossible. Conversely, modern art functions as a conduit of the most meaningless, underdeveloped ideas and moods which find a haven in it. Chaotic and meaningless renditions of the artist's inner confusions are, thus, the very lifeblood of modern art. And, I might add, also the main characters in its low comedy and high insanity.

What indeed compels a person to do this modern art? Based strictly on my observations on the subject, not scientific studies, some common elements seem to suggest a pattern among modern artists.

The modern artist is largely dictated by his *mood* of the moment. Since the dictatorship of the mood requires so little energy and intellect, he can respond to his mood faster than any other person in society, with the exception of a hyperactive child and a psychotic individual. His total existence, hence his total consciousness as an artist, consists of a series of moods, one after another, changing and overlapping into unpredictability and incoherence.

His driving urge for accomplishment is the desire to "express" his fragmented and chaotic emotions. He feels angry, he feels deprived, he feels alienated, he feels heroic—a succession of random mood swings. As these emotions dominate his moments, he wants to tell the world how he "feels." But his feelings come and go, and are ultimately the shapeless and meaningless notions of a child or a lunatic.

His mode of operation is on *impulse*. He takes advantage of the freedom given in modern art but throws that freedom right back into the chains of his own momentous impulse. As a "modern," "avant-garde" artist, he acknowledges no obligation to common reason. Nor does he harness his artistic dynamics with a systematic, orderly inner-discipline. He is full of impulse but knows not how to control it for his ultimate creation. He mistakes his kinetic energy for creative dynamics, and his childish impulse for artistic commitment.

His art is thus a representation of his *psychic* state of mind, not a philosophical public statement. Full of psychic chaos and mood swings, his state of mind lacks depth as philosophy and clarity as art. It is at once meaningless and incomprehensible as it reaches the public domain for inspection. Like the closed group of babbling guru-worshipers, only his inner circle of friends and fellow artists profess to "understand" his art. He complains that the public doesn't care about his art, but does nothing to help the public's better comprehension. For what he calls art amounts little more than to psychoanalysis and pop-psychology. Ordinary viewers are more puzzled by his art than enlightened by what he says.

The modern artist is dominated by immediacy and momentousness, not by a life-long artistic brooding or spiritual searching, both of which are essential to the artist's artistic and personal wholeness and integrity. His personality is more reactive than reflective, more jumpy than dynamic, more hyperactive than productive, more pretentious than committed. As a human being, he is too impatient to reflect, too shallow to master the art of self-discipline. He wants to conquer the world, but is enslaved by his own personal immaturity and inner torments. He wants to be instantaneously famous but lacks the intellectual and spiritual commitment that fame—perhaps not fortune—requires. He is lazy with his artistic mission but overbearing with his artistic claim. He wants to bypass all that is burdensome for an artist and a human being, and go straight to the land of milk and honey.

Finally, the modern artist disdains his public duty as an artist. He recognizes no responsibility for creating and communicating his ideas to the public and posterity. He refuses to acknowledge his own link in the long chain of artistic tradition or an obligation to the art and artists of the past—or what *TIME* magazine calls a "sense of masterpiece"—, whose tradition he is ultimately part of. He looks neither to society nor to art for his commitment and inspiration. All he cares about is his selfish mood of the moment and its quickly-sought fame and fortune. He does so little himself as an artist and a human being, yet he wants so much reward as an artist and a human being. He gives so little, yet demands so much. He desires fame without its virtue; he enjoys freedom without its obligation; he craves the status of an artist without deserving it. Not getting what he feels is his due, he forever pouts and throws tantrums at the world in general.

No wonder, then, the modern artist is thoroughly a creature of commercial hype and a slave to the ebbing and flowing fortunes of chance and luck. What he aims for is not the slow maturation of a complete artist, but a big overnight break with all the attendant benefits of success. If he is not famous now, he reasons, he may get the break tomorrow. If he is famous now, he has "four good years" left, as an artist told Anthony Haden-Guest, in which to make the most of it while it lasts. Sailing with the trendy winds in art fashion, willing to compromise with commercialism for success, the modern artists drifts in his way as an artist and schemes with his art as a mercenary, casting his lot with luck, fortune, and a benevolent hand.

Tom Wolfe tells of how Peggy Guggenheim, one such benevolent hand of modern art, "created" Jackson Pollock: "In a single year, 1943, Peggy Guggenheim [of the Guggenheim Museum] met Pollock, gave him a monthly stipend, got him moving in the direction of Surrealist 'automatic writing' (she loved Surrealism), set him up on Fifty-seventh Street—Uptown Street of Dreams!—with his first show—in the most chic Modernist salon in the history of New York, her own Art of This Century Gallery, with its marvelous Surrealist Room, where the pictures were mounted on baseball bats—got Sweeney to write the catalogue introduction, in prose that ranged from merely rosy to deep purple dreams—and Barr inducted one of the paintings, 'The She Wolf,' into the Museum of Modern Art's Permanent Collection—and Motherwell wrote a rave for *Partisan Review*—and Greenberg wrote a super-rave for *The Nation*...The Consummation was complete and Pollock was a Success before the last painting was hung and the doors were opened and the first Manhattan was poured on opening night."

It is almost wholly accidental that modern art is called art at all. Its more accurate name is children's game, except that its price is no children's game. It is the extraordinary market price that some of its more "successful" works command that gives modern art its most comic and insane character. The possibility of getting millions for an animal-dung artwork boggles every artist's mind and galvanizes every artist to vicious scheming and clever hyping. When one artist's—perhaps Pollock's—incomprehensible nothing is sold for millions, why can't someone else's incomprehensible nothing be sold for millions, since there is no real difference between two incomprehensible nothings? When a large benevolent hand plucks a totally unknown like Pollock and makes him somebody, why can't the same large benevolent hand do the same to another unknown? The artist stays awake at nights with the possibility, his art career or vision taking the back seat to commercial breaks and publicity. His once pure artist's mind is corrupted and is enslaved by the turns of luck and benevolence.

Why wouldn't it, indeed? Unlike classic art in which something resembling something real has to be produced, any child or moron can do modern art. Hence the role of fervent scheming and all-out hyping in modern art. What is presented as modern "art" is perhaps the most chaotic form of shapeless doodling and graphic communication. Unique to modern art, outside the psycho-babbles of druggies and encounter groups, no coherent message is either conveyed by the artist or expected by the public. So, what's in modern art and why should it be done only by so-called qualified artists? The modern artist in many ways is the child who has never grown up, who still draws on the wall and gets praised for it. If we take Andy Warhol and Jackson Pollock as two prototype personalities among modern artists, the infantile and neurotic personality profile of a modern artist is entirely appropriate for his art.

Normal people like us make the transition, as we grow up and face the demands of society, from the sensory to the reflective, from the graphic to the literary, from the emotional to the intellectual, and from internal self-absorption to external reality. True artists—especially those in uncollectible art—refuse to make a total transition from the former state of self and freedom to the latter state of society and public. They achieve a suspended state of balance between self and freedom as essential to artistic creativity and independence, on the one hand, and society and public as essential to the *communication* of their artistic creativity through a public forum, on the other, to be judged and honored. All great artists in all media are a marvelous study in balance between dynamism and control, between internal compulsion and external form, between personal freedom and public necessity—in short, Classicism and Romanticism in balance—, neither side dominating the other thereby destroying the dynamic tension between substance and form in art. Some of us, on the other hand, go all the way to the extreme in our growth and subjugate ourselves wholly to society and public, thereby becoming conformity-minded citizens, rule-bound bureaucrats, and subservient corporate hirelings.

The modern artist, however, is neither in the mold of self-balancing artists that the history of human heritage requires, nor in the mold of tame citizens, bureaucrats, and hirelings that the operation of society requires. They are permanent juveniles who pretend to be artists, refusing to be productive in the ordinary capacities of society. They are, in short, artistic imposters and social parasites: They live off of art without contribution, and are supported by society without performing useful functions. Their so-called art is neither artistic, although it claims to be, nor philosophical, although it claims to be. Nothing useful can be made out of its art-ness, and nothing intelligible gleaned from its message. What passes for "an artist's personality" is really a cover for one who is undisciplined intellectually, chaotic in thought formation, and underdeveloped in personal growth. He is still the child with crayons and a wall. No wonder that all modern art forms are derivatives of "Impressionism," the art of recording impressions, at once vague and incomplete. If we could only imagine "impressionist" plays, novels, symphonies, or philosophical ideas!

I am not sure if anything different, more whole or more complete, can be expected or produced out of collectable art in general and modern art in particular—even under the best of circumstances. If the artist were thoroughly mature with his person, clearly articulate with his artistic philosophy, and fully skilled as a craftsman, *could* he possibly be a collectable artist, much less a modern artist? His verbally stated aim and philosophy of art—as we read them here and there—are so incoherent that they surely rank among the lowest and most unintelligible of human utterances. How can one "paint" something clearly that one cannot articulate clearly in one's thought?

However, there is one major function in modern art that most people, even critics and experts, seem to overlook. It is its "therapeutic value." In other words, modern art is the poorman's psychiatrist. Through its free modes of expression, its tolerance for deviant behavior, and its expectation of juvenile intellect, modern art performs the marvelous function of psychotherapy for the befuddled, the confused, and the fixated. In fact, art—largely modernistic art—is a legitimate method of therapy that is academically recognized and established. The modern artist colony—typically in Greenwich Village—may be thought of as a large out-patient clinic where the patients are engaged in self-therapy. The drawings they make on the canvas are wonderful tools for psychiatrists who want to look into the states of their minds and the weird way their minds work. If a traveller from outer space landed in one of the modern art colonies and saw the pictures, the alien's instinctive reaction would be that they are all crazy. If the outer space traveller read the utterances by Robert Henri, the founder of the "Ash Can" school of modern art, he would surely think it, for all its pseudo-philosophy, equivalent to psychedelic drug experience. It is indeed the marvel of modern comedy and insanity in marketing that some of these therapeutic objects are picked up as great works of art to the tune of millions of dollars.

Are we still to call modern "art" art and the modern "artist" artist? We detest opaqueness in everything else we do in society. We hate unclear statements in daily conversations, in scholarship, in legal language, in business contracts, and so on as ridiculous and obtuse. Yet we not only accept but expect such opaque and abstract nonsense in modern art. But why? I think it is precisely because so-called modern art has become a nonentity both as art and as philosophy. The world has learned to expect just about anything from modern art, which is to say, nothing in particular. With the granting of this immunity, perhaps more seriously, modern art has also been branded with the stamp of irrelevance. Like a pretty picture on the wall that no one specially notices, modern art matters none in the scheme of life. The public by and large has decided that it is utter nonsense and stopped paying attention to that particular art form.

First, modern art has become irrelevant technically. It cannot compete with handsome illustrations and photographs for realism. Its works, being neither pretty nor functional, are inferior in usefulness to landscape art and interior decoration, for they suffer by turns public revulsion, indifference, and ridicule. Modern art is closer to a hobby than art: Both are forms of self-indulgence; both are devoid of serious purpose; both are unspecific and vague in conception; both are carried out with typically low energy-concentration. The only difference, however, perhaps a significant one, is that some modern artworks cost in the millions.

Then, modern art has also become irrelevant substantively. Its pseudo-serious intellectual musings are far inferior to those of "real" intellectuals in philosophy, journalism, literature, or social criticism. In the completeness of the art form, it is nowhere near the wholeness and coherence of *un*collectible art forms. A modern artwork is at best equivalent to a bar in music, a few words in literature, less than a footnote in philosophy. The modern artist, however, tries to make up with elaborate and empty theories, concepts, and approaches what he lacks in substance. Every modern artist by necessity has become a theorist of his art—and his art a "painted word"—, for his empty art-philosophy has to be made up in words, and more often in bizarre antics, shock methods, and the increasing strangeness in its subject and expression.

How this juvenile exercise—confusing, incomplete, unfocused—not only exists on such a scale but also prospers in the name of art, costing millions of dollars and occupying places of honor in public museums and private collections, is perhaps the most supremely ridiculous cultural phenomenon in Western civilization. Could any other low comedy or high insanity possibly match it?

I think not.

Bibliography

REFERENCE

BOOKS

L. Aagaard-Mogensen, *CULTURE AND ART: AN ANTHOLOGY*. Humanities Press, Atlantic Highlands, NJ. 1976.

Laurie Adams, *ART ON TRIAL: WHISTLER TO ROTHKO*. Walker, New York. 1976.

Frank Arnau, *THE ART OF THE FAKER: THREE THOUSAND YEARS OF DECEPTION*. Little, Brown, Boston. 1961.

Denis Dutton (ed), *THE FORGER'S ART*. Univ. of Calif. Press, Berkeley, CA. 1983.

Stuart J. Flemming, *AUTHENTICITY IN ART: THE SCIENTIFIC DETECTION OF FORGERY*. Crane, Russack, New York. 1975.

John Godley, *THE MASTER FORGER: THE STORY OF HAN VAN MEEGEREN*. Wilfred Funk, New York. 1950.

Ian Haywood, *FAKING IT: ART AND THE POLITICS OF FORGERY*. St. Martin's, Boston. 1987.

Clifford Irvin, *FAKE*, McGraw Hill, New York. 1969.

H.W. Janson, *THE PICTURE HISTORY OF PAINTING*. Harry N. Abrams, New York. 1957.

Lawrence Jeppson, *FABULOUS FRAUDS*. Arlington Books, London. 1970.

K.E. Meyer, *THE PLUNDERED PAST: THE TRAFFIC IN ART TREASURES*. Penguin Books, London. 1977.

Geraldine Norman and Tom Keating, *THE FAKE'S PROGRESS: TOM KEATING'S STORY*. Hutchinson, London. 1977.

M. Roskill, *WHAT IS ART HISTORY?*. Harper and Row, New York. 1976.

S. Sachs, *FAKES AND FORGERIES*. Minneapolis Institute of Arts, Minneapolis, Minnesota. 1973.

George Savage, *FORGERIES, FAKES, AND REPRODUCTIONS*. Barrie & Rockliff, London. 1963.

Hans Tietze, *GENUINE AND FALSE: COPIES, IMITATIONS, FORGERIES*. Chanticleer Press, New York. 1948.

Ann Waldron, *TRUE OR FALSE? AMAZING ART FORGERIES*. Hastings House, New York. 1983.

Tom Wolfe, *THE PAINTED WORD*. Farrar, Straus and Giroux, New York. 1975.

Robert Wraight, *THE ART GAME AGAIN*. Leslie Frewin, London. 1974.

Christopher Wright, *THE ART OF THE FORGER*. Dodd, Mead, New York. 1985.

ARTICLES

M.P. Battin, "Exact replication in the visual arts," *J OF AESTHETICS AND ART CRITICISM*, vol 38, pt 2 (Winter 1979) 153-8.

K. Bazarov, "Emperors with no clothes," *ART AND ARTISTS* (UK), vol 12, pt 4 (July 1977) 34-6.

S.J. Checkland, "The Tom Keating saga," *ARTS REVIEW* (UK), vol 31, pt 5 (16 March 1979) p. 110, 112, 133.

Lord Clark, "Forgeries," *HISTORY TODAY* (UK), vol 29, pt 11 (1979) 724-33.

T. Del Renzio, "Multiple authenticity," *ART AND ARTISTS* 2 (UK), vol 9, pt 4 (July 1974).

D. Dutton, "Artistic crimes: the problem of forgery in the arts," *B J OF AESTHETICS*, vol 19, pt 4 (autumn 1979) 302-14.

A. Elsen, "Art replicas: a question of ethics," *ARTNEWS*, vol 78, pt 2 (Feb 1979).

P. Failing, "The Degas bronzes Degas never knew," *ARTNEWS*, vol 78, pt 4 (April 1979).

P. Fuller, "Forgeries," *ART MONTHLY* (UK) no 1 (Oct 1976) 7-9.

P. Gilmour, "The art of reproduction," *ARTS REVIEW* (UK), vol 31, pt 4 (2 March 1979).

G. Glueck, "The experts' guide to the experts," *ARTNEWS*, vol 77, pt 9 (Nov 1978).

M. Haggerty, "The Italian market," *ART MONTHLY* (UK), no 26 (May 1979) 5-7.

S. Hochfield, "Problems in the reproduction of sculpture," *ARTNEWS*, vol 73, pt 9 (Nov 1974) 20-9.

_____ "The Watercolorgate affair," *ARTNEWS*, vol 75, pt 8 (Oct 1976) 49-50.

H. Katzander, "Say goodbye to the caveat emptor," *ARTS MAGAZINE*, vol 48, pt 2 (Nov 1973) 74-5.

W. E. Kennick, "Art and inauthenticity," in *J OF AESTHETICS AND ART CRITICISM*, vol 44, pt 1 (fall 1985) 3-12.

T. Kulka, "The artistic and aesthetic status of forgeries," in *LEONARDO* (UK), vol 15, pt 2 (spring 1982), 115-17, summary of English.

_____ "The artistic and the aesthetic value of art," in *BRITISH JOURNAL OF AESTHETICS*, vol 21, pt 4 (autumn 1981) 336-50.

I. MacKenzie, "Gadamer's hermeneutics and the uses of forgery," *J OF AESTHETICS AND ART CRITICISM*, vol 45, pt 1 (fall 1986) 42-8.

J. Margolis, "Aesthetic appreciation and the imperceptible," *B J OF AESTHETICS*, vol 16, pt (autumn 1976) 305-12.

E. Maurer, "Caveat Ethnos: unmasking frauds in ethnographic art," *NATIONAL ARTS GUIDE*, vol 3, pt 2 (March-April 1981) 22-5.

G. McFee, "Adam made me," *B J OF AESTHETICS*, vol 18, pt. 4 (autumn 1978) 373-7.

A. McIntyre, "Fake Pollocks fool Australian art establishment," *ART MONTHLY* (UK), no 18 (July-Aug 1978) 4-6.

J.H. Merryman and R. Duffy, "Art and the law," *ART JOURNAL*, vol 34, pt 4 (summer 1975) 332-6.

G. Rosolato, "Psychoanalytic notes on the theft and defacement of works of art," *MUSEUM* (France), vol 26, pt 1 (1974) 21-5.

M. Sagoff, "On the aesthetic and economic value of art," *B J OF AESTHETICS*, vol 21, pt 4 (autumn 1981) 318-29.

_____ "The aesthetic status of forgeries," *J OF AESTHETICS AND ART CRITICISM*, vol 35, pt 2 (winter 1976) 169-80.

H. Steele, "Fakes and forgeries," *B J OF AESTHETICS*, vol 17, pt 3 (summer 1977) 254-8.

M. Stevens, "Retouching Rembrandt," *THE NEW REPUBLIC*, (Aug 22, 1988) 28-31.

V.G. Swanson, "Lawrence Alma-Tadema: his forgers and his imitators," *NINETEENTH CENTURY*. vol 3, pt 4 (winter 1977) 66-70.

V. Thorson, "Reassessing Rodin's graphics," *ARTNEWS*, vol 74, pt 7 (Sept 1975) 40-2, 46.

M Vermeulen, "The case of the curious Cassatt, or elementary my dear Watson," *NEW ART EXAMINER*, vol 4, pt 8 (May 1977) p. 1, 8.

F. Willet, "True or False? The false dichotomy," *AFRICAN ARTS*, vol 9, pt 3 (April 1976) 8-14.

M. Wykes-Joyce, "Forgers in perspective," *ARTS REVIEW* (UK), vol 28, pt 19 (17 Sept 1976) p. 485, 487.

Index

"A Day at the Studio," 154
Adams, Laurie, 34, 50, 77, 111
aesthetic value (judgement), 2, 25,
  38, 51-52, 60-61, 101, 104, 116-117,
  121, 142, 149
African art, 80, 89, 99
Agnew's, 14
"Ann Landers," 119
anonymous authorship, 131
anti-art, 50
archaeology, 19
Arnau, Frank, 82, 92, 109, 111
art:
  and craftsmanship, 147
  and money, 129, 134-136
  as fraud, 71
  as graphic representation, 143-144
  as hoax, 74, 77-78, 81, 89, 99,
  102, 136, 164
  as unexpertisable, 21
  beauty and, 2, 24, 29-30, 34-36,
  38, 39-40, 49, 101-102, 130,
  147, 149
  big-name philosophy in, 47-52
  consumption of, 46-47
  corruption of, 135-136
  definition of, 34-35, 75, 86
  dispute (scandal), 20, 38, 45,
  102, 127-128
  "Earth," 153
  fame and fortune in, 133-135
  "Illogic-Incoherent," 155
  "Impossible," 153
  major, 2-3
  metaphor, 146
  "Micro Emotive," 153
  minor, 2-3
  mystery in, 2, 4, 18, 25, 28,
  32, 48, 70, 81, 95, 137
  "nothing" as, 2-3, 25-26,

  71-72, 74, 78, 84, 92-93, 96,
  100-101, 136, 139-141,
  143-144, 155
  ownership (possession) of, 2,
  33, 35-37, 41-43, 49, 52, 65,
  95, 107, 120-121, 128, 142
  purpose of, 107-108
  "Possible," 153
  rarity of, 147, 149
  therapy, 87, 163
art business, 3-4, 10, 21, 24,
  26, 37, 47, 49, 94-95
art collection, 1, 10, 33-35,
  39-41, 43-44, 48, 50, 117,
  120-121
art expert:
  authority, 28, 137
  becoming, 19-21
  compared with psychiatry, 31-32
  confusion and contradiction, 17,
  23, 30, 106, 112
  dilemmas, 12-18, 22
  incompetence, 16, 18, 20-21, 94
  in general, 3, 7-8, 11
  majority view of, 98
  minority view of, 98
  nature of art expertise, 18,
  21, 84
art establishment, 2, 7, 10-11,
  16, 72, 98, 101-102, 128, 136
art-hating, 42-44, 50, 120, 140
art history, 19, 37-38, 52, 89,
  145
art market, 32, 35, 46-48, 54,
  75-76, 78-81, 84, 103, 114-118,
  120, 122, 126, 136
art response, 2, 100-101,
  137-138, 141-143
art scholarship, 37-38
"Ash Can School," 163

168

www.ingramcontent.com/pod-product-compliance
Lightning Source LLC
Chambersburg PA
CBHW031048180526
45163CB00002BA/737